GLOBETROTTER

The CYPRUS

PAUL HARCOURT DAVIES

NEW
HOLLAND

GLOBETROTTER™

Second edition published in 2006
by New Holland Publishers (UK) Ltd
London • Cape Town • Sydney • Auckland
First published in 2002

10 9 8 7 6 5 4 3 2

website: www.newhollandpublishers.com

Garfield House, 86 Edgware Road
London W2 2EA
United Kingdom

80 McKenzie Street
Cape Town 8001
South Africa

Unit 1, 66 Gibbes Street
Chatswood, NSW 2067
Australia

218 Lake Road
Northcote, Auckland
New Zealand

Distributed in the USA by
The Globe Pequot Press, Connecticut

ISBN 978 1 84537 434 1

Publishing Manager (UK): Simon Pooley
Publishing Manager (SA): Thea Grobbelaar
DTP Cartographic Manager: Genené Hart
Editors: Thea Grobbelaar, Jacqueline de Villiers
Designers: Nicole Bannister, Lellyn Creamer
Cartographer: Nicole Bannister
Updated by: Robin Gauldie

Reproduction by Resolution (Cape Town) and
Hirt & Carter (Pty) Ltd, Cape Town
Printed and bound by Times Offset (M) Sdn. Bhd.,
Malaysia.

CONTENTS

MAKE THE MOST OF YOUR GUIDE

Reading these two pages will help you to get the most out of your guide and save you time when using it. Sites discussed in the text are cross-referenced with the cover maps – for example, the reference 'Map F–B2' refers to the Lefkosia Map (Map F), column B, row 2. Use the Map Plan below to quickly locate the map you need.

MAP PLAN

Outside Back Cover   Outside Front Cover

Inside Front Cover   Inside Back Cover

THE BIGGER PICTURE

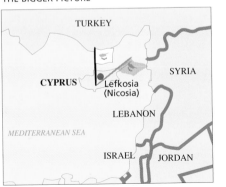

Key to Map Plan

A – Pafos
B – Ancient Kourion
C – Lemesos
D – Lemesos Beach
E – Cyprus
F – Lefkosia
G – Larnaka
H – Larnaka Beach
I – Paralimni
J – Agia Napa Area
K – Troödos Mountains
L – Excursions

USING THIS BOOK

Key to Symbols

⊠ — address   ⌂ — e-mail address

☎ — telephone   ⊕ — opening times

𝄭 — fax   𝖉 — entry fee

▪ — website   ❗◧ — restaurants nearby

Map Legend

motorway	▬▬▬	main road	Posidonos
national road	▬▬▬	other road	Priamou
main road	▬▬▬	built-up area	
minor road	▬▬▬	wall	
track	▬▬▬	ferry	– – –
river	(vadi)	hotel	(H) CLEOPATRA
city	**LEFKOSIA (NICOSIA)**	police station	●
town	O Aglangia	hospital	⊕
large village	◎ Paralimni	library	⌓
village	O Troödos	place of interest	● Cyprus Archaeological Musem
peak in metres	Chionista (Mt Olympus) ▲ 1952 m	parking	🅿
airport	✈ ✈	place of worship	△ Agios Lazaros
ruin	∴	tourist information	ⓘ
viewpoint	⊻	post office	⊠
water sports	Ⓦ	bus terminus	🚌
diving	⤜	park & garden	
beach	‿		

Keep us Current

Travel information is apt to change, which is why we regularly update our guides. We'd be most grateful to receive feedback from you if you've noted something we should include in our updates. If you have any new information, please share it with us by writing to the Publishing Manager, Globetrotter, at the office nearest to you (addresses on the imprint page of this guide). The most significant contribution to each new edition will be rewarded with a free copy of the updated guide.

Above: *The Kariotis near Kakopetria becomes a torrent when swollen by melting snow from Troödos.*

CYPRUS

Cyprus, **Aphrodite's Isle**, is strategically located at the eastern end of the Mediterranean. It has long been fought over by its many conquerors, from the **Phoenicians** to the **Greeks**, the **Romans** and the **Ottoman Turks**. Its turbulent history, and the rich and varied cultures of those who have ruled it over the centuries, have left their mark everywhere. The island is a huge **archaeological site**, in which treasures still lie waiting to be discovered.

The Land
Climate

Two mountain ranges influence the climate and the high level of **sunshine** creates considerable temperature differences (both seasonal and day to night) between land and sea. Western coastal areas tend to have slightly cooler summers and milder winters than the interior. The climate is classed as '**arid Mediterranean**', though there is more seasonal variety.

Plant Life

The island hosts 1800 species of flowering plants, among them over 120 endemics, including several **orchids**. In spring there is a riot of colourful **shrubs**, **annuals** (such as poppies and crown daisies) and **bulbs**, including narcissus, crocus and tulips. The forests on the heights of Troödos consist of black pine, ancient juniper and planted Cyprus cedar. At lower altitudes the woods are denser, mainly of Calabrian pine with an under-storey of Cyprus golden oak (*Quercus alniifolia*) and red-barked eastern strawberry tree (*Arbutus andrachne*). Oranges, lemons, olives and almonds are grown all over the island and in February and March, the fields are a sea of pale pink as the almond trees blossom.

Climate

Hot dry summers from June to September and variable winters from November until February/March are separated by a short spring and autumn. Choose spring for flowers, walk in spring and autumn, sizzle on the beach in summer and ski in Troödos in winter.

Wildlife

The largest mammal is the **moufflon**. **Foxes** occur in Akamas, and Cyprus **hares** survive in small populations. The island has its own races of **shrew** and **spiny mouse**. Eight bat species are recorded. Birdwatchers may see the best known endemic **bird**, the Cyprus warbler. Plankton levels and consequently **fish** numbers are on the low side, although some 200 species of fish have been documented in the sea around Cyprus. **Butterflies** are the most obviously attractive of the island's insects. Green and Loggerhead **turtles** lay their eggs on secluded Lara Beach on the Akamas Peninsula. Environmentalists have set up a study centre here to hatch the babies under cover, where they will not be damaged by tourists or predators. In this way some 4000 turtles are successfully hatched here every year.

> **Hedgehogs**
> The **long-eared hedgehog** has had an unhappy time in Cyprus since local superstition gave it a reputation for clambering into chicken coops, intent on having its spiny way with the hens. Physical improbability did not deter the population in their persecution of the innocent creature.

History in Brief

Although the first settlers are thought to have voyaged from **Asia Minor**, people have lived in Cyprus for at least 9000 years. By about 2000BC copper began to be exported from Cyprus. Around 1300BC, the island was culturally enriched by the Achaean Greeks from the northern Peloponnese, who brought with them their **Mycenaean** language and religious traditions. But the 1050BC earthquakes destroyed Enkomi and other **Bronze Age** settlements.

Below: The Sanctuary of Apollo Hylates near Lemesos.

The City Kingdoms

After a long isolation, the island's trade revived when **Phoenicians** established a settlement in Kition in the 8th century BC. Many other city kingdoms were also established. By 700BC, the rulers of the city kingdoms had submitted to King Sargon II of **Assyria**. On the fall of the Assyrian Empire, rule passed first to the Egyptians in 560BC and then the Persians in 545.

The Hellenistic Period

From 475 to 325BC, the island of Cyprus remained a naval base under Persian rule. Alexander the Great secured the unanimous support of the Kings of Cyprus in his campaign against the Persians, and after his victory Cyprus became part of his Hellenistic empire. Following Alexander's death in 323BC, Cyprus became a pawn in the squabbles between his generals, Ptolemy and Antigonus. **Ptolemy** prevailed and Cyprus became thoroughly Hellenized and essentially a province of Egypt, important for its copper, timber, shipbuilding, corn and wine, with Pafos as its capital.

Pax Romana and Byzantium

In 58BC, Cyprus was annexed by **Rome**, thereby becoming a senatorial province. A long era of peace and stability began. **Christianity** was declared the official religion in AD323, though adoption of the new faith spread slowly.

When the Roman Empire was split in two in AD395, Cyprus came under Byzantine rule from the eastern capital, Constantinople. During the 7th century the coastal towns were plagued by **Arab raiders** until, in 688, a treaty between Emperor Justinian II and Caliph al-Malik effectively neutralized the island. Cyprus flourished in the Middle Byzantine period (965–1185), and many towns were either founded or enlarged.

Below: *Petra tou Romiou, birthplace of Aphrodite, is named after the giant Romios, said to have thrown the great rocks at Arab pirates.*

The Lusignans and the Venetians

The despotic Isaac Comnenos declared independence from Constantinople in 1184 and began a seven-year rule characterized by greed and cruelty. In 1191 he was overthrown by Richard the Lionheart. Richard sold the island to Guy de Lusignan, who instituted the feudal system,

and thus began a wonderful period for the Frankish nobility. Between 1374 and 1464 Famagusta was occupied by the Genoese whose attack on the island crippled it economically. The last Lusignan monarch, James II, married Venetian Caterina Cornaro in 1472. She succeeded him and so began a period of Venetian rule characterized by even more oppressive taxation.

Ottoman Rule

The Venetians regarded Cyprus as a frontier fortress against the threat from Ottoman forces; the decisive attack came in 1570, when Lefkosia (Nicosia) fell after a 7-week siege – with half its population slaughtered. Famagusta held out for 10 months until July 1571. Over the next three centuries, Muslim and Christian peasants united often in **revolt** against punitive taxation and neglect.

The British

In the face of 19th-century Russian expansionism, Britain guaranteed to protect the Ottoman Empire under the Anglo-Turkish Convention of 1878. Cyprus was leased to Britain. Turkey supported Germany in World War I, and Britain decided to annex the island, eventually declaring it a **Crown Colony** in 1925.

Above: *The beautiful Venetian monastery of Agia Napa is built near a spring where there had been a settlement since the Hellenistic period.*
Below: *The statue of Archbishop Makarios III stands outside the Archbishop's Palace in old Lefkosia.*

Above: *The Green Line is a continuing reminder that this is, more than two decades on, still a divided island.*

As the economy grew from the early 1930s, so did demands for an end to British rule and for *énosis* – unity with Greece. **Makarios**, the elected Bishop of Kition in 1950, became a powerful advocate of *énosis*. However, after the Suez crisis of 1954 Britain became even more determined to hang on to Cyprus, its 'unsinkable aircraft carrier'. Turkey and Greece threatened to go to war, but the USA exerted pressure on both sides to find a diplomatic solution. Makarios abandoned his claim for *énosis* and Cyprus gained **independence** but with an unsatisfactory constitution.

Northern Enclaves
Following partition in 1974, a small Greek community was allowed to remain in **Rizokarpaso** on the Karpas Peninsula, but conditions have been made difficult – anyone leaving is not allowed to return. The Maronites are descendants of an ancient Christian sect originating in Syria. They remained neutral in the struggle between Greek Orthodox and Turkish Muslim Cypriots, and in theory they are allowed to remain in the north. In practice, property has been appropriated, schools have been closed and almost everyone between the ages of 12 and 45 has emigrated. Older Maronites can visit the south for only five days at a time.

Republic of Cyprus
The constitution gave the minority Turkish population disproportionate representation and an uneasy peace existed until 1963, when Makarios proposed constitutional changes. Fighting broke out in Lefkosia and the Turkish Cypriots retreated into enclaves; the Greeks imposed a trade embargo, lifted in 1968.

As matters within Cyprus calmed, its relations with Athens worsened. Greek interests in America whipped up criticism of Makarios and Greek military attacked the presidential palace on 15 July 1974. On 20 July the Turks bombed Lefkosia and landed troops on the northern coast, and two days later the Greek Colonels fell from power in Athens. In August 1974 the Turkish army seized some 37% of the island in **Operation Attila** and an economic crisis hit the south, which faced 40% unemployment. Bloody reprisals were inflicted on the Turks in the south, while thousands of Greek Cypriots were taken prisoner.

Modern Cyprus

The **Turkish-occupied north** has languished in poverty and corruption since the invasion of 1974, while the legitimate **Republic of Cyprus in the south** has flourished. In 2005, Cyprus joined the EU, after a UN-sponsored, island-wide referendum in which Turkish Cypriots voted in favour of a reunited Cyprus. Greek Cypriots felt differently and rejected reunification. Cyprus remains divided, and the occupied north is recognized as a state only by Turkey.

Government and Economy

Since 1974, **Greek Cypriots** have worked to regenerate their economy. The population is highly educated and unemployment is under 2 per cent. The standard of health and health care is very high; figures for life expectancy and child mortality compare favourably with any western country.

The key to the early success of the south was **tourism**; the government played the refugee card for all it was worth to attract money from outside the island. Cyprus has become popular with Germans, Scandinavians and increasingly, visitors from Russia and Eastern Europe, although Britain remains the largest market. Since 1974 there has been growth in light industry and manufacturing. An influx of wealthy escapees from strife-torn Lebanon meant that Cyprus became the base for many companies in the Middle East. Nowadays there is a large cohort of 'offshore' companies, and the accounting and banking expertise required to service them. The British

> **Emigrants**
> Compared with Greek Cypriots, a high proportion of Turkish Cypriots emigrated following the invasion of 1974. About 100,000 Turkish Cypriots still live in the north, but an estimated 300,000 live in Britain, America, Australia and Turkey. A result of the invasion is that the Turks, some 18 per cent of the population, occupy 37 per cent of the land area.

Below: *A roadside orange seller in Pafos.*

Different Faiths
Among the resident population of about 650,000, religious adherence is divided. Some 84 per cent of the people are members of the Greek Orthodox church, 14 per cent are Muslims, and the remaining two per cent are Maronite, Armenian or Catholic.

Opposite: *The tradition of icon painting is preserved at Trooditissa where monks still live in the monastery high in the Troödos Mountains, surrounded by pines and well-tended orchards.*
Below: *Playing tavli, or backgammon. The intermittent click of the dice punctuates conversation at every Cypriot café.*

army retains a presence on Cyprus, and there are two bases: one between Lemesos and Pafos, and one on the road to Agia Napa.

The People

Thanks to a long and chequered history, Cypriots do not fall into definite racial categories so much as into groups distinguished by their linguistic and religious allegiances. The various different elements within the population – Greeks, Latins and Turks – have always mixed and matched. Both **Turkish** and **Greek** Cypriots are quite different from their respective mainland counterparts, but are very much like each other in terms of warmth and **hospitality**.

Education

Compulsory school begins at five and a half, often followed immediately by private lessons in English and other languages. The work ethic is strong in Cypriot children. Entry to the **Gymnasium** is at 11, followed by a division after three years into academic and technical streams. There are private international schools in all the main towns. These cater for children of all nationalities and prepare them for entry into both British and American universities. The insatiable thirst for qualifica-

tions has spawned an industry in 'crammers' (*frontisteria*). The **University of Cyprus** opened in 1992 and has an excellent reputation, though many students go abroad to study, since Cyprus is too small an island to provide enough employment for highly qualified professionals.

Family Life

The importance of the **family** over-rides everything else to a Cypriot. Ties are strong and consequently people feel they matter to one another, and crime levels are very low. Cypriots genuinely love **children** and cannot understand the reports they read of child abuse elsewhere. The extended family is vital in enabling many professional women in Cyprus to continue their careers, leaving their children under the wing of 'Yia-ya' (grandmother) and their aunts.

Religion

Religion is important in Cyprus but is not a contentious issue. The south is Greek Orthodox and the north Sunni Muslim, but within both areas are other religious adherences as well as secular groups. In many southern villages a familiar sight is the priest, sitting in the local café – pivotal in the community and aware of everything, good and bad, among his flock.

Architecture

The architectural legacy of past times is evident in all the major towns: **Byzantine** churches and fortifications were expanded by **Lusignan** rulers, fortified by the **Venetians** and then rebuilt by the Ottoman **Turks**. The main towns and cities have all suffered from the use and abuse of the 'great god concrete', particularly following the invasion, when planning controls may have existed but were not implemented. Sadly, many fine old houses have disappeared, though some Ottoman and early colonial buildings have survived.

Icons

Icons have always held a central place in the Orthodox Church. In Cyprus, worship of the Madonna replaced obeisance to Aphrodite, and images of the Virgin and Child are common. Richly decorated with gold leaf, the paintings are highly prized by collectors. Several monasteries were founded where miraculous icons (often painted by St Luke) had reputedly been discovered, usually revealing themselves by sounds and a preternatural glow. During the 8th and 9th centuries the worship of icons was declared idolatrous and many were destroyed. In Cyprus it is still customary to kiss icons.

✪ *See* Map E–A4   ★★★

Orchids
Many orchid enthusiasts visit Cyprus in spring, finding here a unique assemblage of species which could otherwise only be found by making several journeys much further afield. These include bee orchids, three of which are endemic: **Kotschyi's ophrys**, the **Lapithos ophrys** and the **elegant ophrys**. Later in the year, the Troödos has its own **Troödos helleborine** and, in a few wet places, the rare **eastern marsh helleborine**.

AKAMAS

The isolated, unspoiled area of Akamas supports a wealth of rare plants, the Cyprus tulip (*Tulipa cypria*), orchids such as the very rare *Orchis punctulata* and small insect mimics (*Ophrys*) among them. Some plants have evolved over the millennia during which this area has been isolated to become quite distinct species endemic to the region. Several plants restricted to Akamas show this in their scientific names, such as the tiny yellow-flowered Akamas Alyssum (*Alyssum akamassicum*) and a member of the thistle family, the pink Akamas Centaury (*Centaurea akamantis*).

The sandy beaches at **Lara** attract both green and loggerhead **turtles** which haul themselves laboriously ashore from late May into August to lay their eggs – reputedly on moonlit nights. Aware that large numbers of tourists and nesting sites for these animals do not mix, the conservation-minded Fisheries Department has waged a determined battle against development. Nests are located and the eggs, buried deep in the sand, are protected by a wire cage. The hatchlings are removed by patrols and taken to the sea in the evening safe from wandering foxes, their main predators. Empty eggshells, like broken ping-pong balls, can sometimes be found along the beach.

Below: *Isolated and, as yet, unspoiled, Akamas attracts discerning visitors.*

⭐ *See* Map A–A3 ★★★

PAFOS HARBOUR AND CASTLE

Pafos Tourism Office
✉ Gladstonos 3,
CY 8046 Pafos
☎ 26 93 28 41
🕐 08:15–14:30 and
15:00–18:30 Mon–Sat;
closed on Wed and Sat
afternoons.

Castle
🕐 09:00–17:00 daily
in winter, 09:00–18:00
daily in summer
✉ Pafos harbour
entrance
💰 CY£0.75

Left: *The fort
guarding Pafos
harbour.*

Pafos's bustling **harbour** has retained its appeal, with many fish restaurants and a tame pelican strutting along the waterfront. It is filled with colourful fishing boats and tour boats, and its tavernas – although not the best in Pafos – are popular and atmospheric. You can still see the ancient breakwaters which once sheltered Greek and Roman vessels.

The small **castle** stands on the harbour breakwater, on the site of earlier castles dating back to ancient times. Guarding the harbour entrance, it is all that remains of a larger Lusignan building constructed in 1391. It was demolished by the Venetians to prevent its use by invading Turks, and then restored and strengthened under Ottoman rule after the island was captured. There are boat trips (excursions in a glass-bottomed boat) which travel from the harbour to Lara and various other places around Akamas.

Early Convert
The Apostles Paul and Barnabas visited Pafos in AD47 and succeeded in converting Sergius Paulus, the Proconsul at the time, to the new faith of Christianity. However, they achieved this success only after the locals had made sure Paul suffered for his beliefs: the church of **Agia Kyriaki** contains the pillar against which he is said to have received 39 lashes.

Above: *The theatre in its imposing setting is Kourion's best known feature – concerts and plays are staged here throughout the summer.*

Ancient Kourion
✉ 19km (11.8 miles) west of Lemesos on the road to Pafos
🕐 08:00–19:30 daily in summer, 08:00–17:00 daily in winter
☎ 25 99 50 48
💰 CY£1.00

Sanctuary
✉ About 2km (1.2 miles) west of Kourion
☎ 25 99 50 49
🕐 09:00–19:30 daily (09:00–17:00 Oct–Apr)
💰 CY£0.75

Kourion Museum
✉ Episkopi, 14km (8.7 miles) west of Lemesos
☎ 25 93 24 53
🕐 09:00–14:30 Mon–Fri and 15:00–17:00 Thu, Sep–Jun
💰 CY£0.75

🌀 *See* Map B	★★★

KOURION (CURIUM)

The ruins of ancient **Kourion**, which stand in memorable splendour high above the sea, are spread over three separate sites. The visible remains date from the **Hellenistic** (Mycenaean and Dorian), **Roman** and **early Christian** periods. Traces of the earlier city kingdom of Kourion have eluded discovery.

The western part of the site includes a basilica said to have been commissioned by Bishop Zeno in the 5th century. It is less impressive than the atrium next to it, which has mosaics and the remains of columns. Unfortunately large parts of the site are off-limits because of excavation work.

The **stadium** once sat 6000 people in seven tiers. Along its southern wall runs what remains of the aqueduct which carried water from the mountains to the city of Kourion. The Christian basilica to the east of the stadium seems to have been built to replace a pagan temple: in 1974, marble slabs on the floor were found to have come from the nymphaeum and to have been strategically placed to cover pagan scenes in earlier mosaics.

Tracing the path of the aqueduct to the west leads to the **Sanctuary of Apollo Hylates**, dominating a small hill. The extant remains are from an early Roman building, damaged in an earthquake in AD365. However, worship on this site began as early as the 7th century BC: the deity Apollo Hylates was a fusion of the imported Greek god Apollo with a local woodland god.

See Map E–F4 ★★★

HALA SULTAN TEKKE

Across Larnaka's salt lake and situated amongst palm trees, is the picturesque **Tekke**, or Hala Sultana Tekkesi. It is a Muslim shrine, that was built in 1816 over the tomb of **Umm Haram**, allegedly an aunt of Prophet Mohammed. The mosque ranks as the third most important in Muslim culture after Mecca and Medina.

Prophet Mohammed's aunt accompanied her husband in the Arab invasion of AD674, but fell from her mule and broke her neck. She was buried on this spot and, more recently, in 1930, Chadija, grandmother of King Hussein of Jordan, was also buried here. In springtime, the secondary grassland and the open pine plantations to the west of the Tekke are the home of many species of wild orchid which flower from January to April.

The Salt Lake
In winter and spring the extensive basins near Lanarka airport fill with salt water as it permeates the porous rocks which separate them from the sea. In summer the water evaporates and leaves a **salt crust**, which is still collected as it has been since Lusignan times, though now on a much smaller scale. In winter, **flamingoes** arrive and make the lake their home until March or April.

Left: *The Hala Sultan Tekke, an important shrine in the Muslim world.*

Hala Sultan Tekke
⊕ 09:00–17:00 daily (07:30–19:30 in summer)
✉ Dromolaxia, on the banks of the Salt Lake, 5km (3 miles) west of Larnaka.
💰 CY£0.75

See Map J–C1   ★★

Beaches
Beaches around the southeast corner of the island are very good, with the fine white sand sought after by holiday-makers. In summer the beaches around Agia Napa get very crowded and should be avoided by those seeking peace and quiet. A wide range of water sports is available.

PROTARAS

Agia Napa is packed with hotels, tourist shops, restaurants and cafés. With guaranteed sunshine, tourists and locals can visit the beaches and take part in water sports of every description. The beaches here used to have comparatively few visitors, other than those staying in Varosha who decided to explore further south. Since 1974, however, this area has seen more development than any other on the island, and it caters for those holiday-makers who want sun, sea and hotel-based entertainment.

Only a few years ago Protaras was just **Fig Tree Bay** – a long stretch of sand, gently sloping to a crystal-clear sea, named after the fig tree at the café claimed to have been brought from the east in the 17th century. The calm water and long run along the coast make it a favourite venue for **water-skiers**, while an offshore island affords some escape for swimmers from the beaches which can get crowded in summer. The speed at which the town has grown is scarcely credible, and the strip of wall-to-wall hotels makes it difficult for non-residents to find the beach. Those who enjoy snorkelling or swimming off a rocky coast will find **Cape Greko** attractive when the sea is calm.

Below: *With its abundance of hotels, Protaras epitomizes sun and fun in Fig Tree Bay.*

See Map F–C4 ★★

THE ARCHBISHOP'S PALACE AND CATHEDRAL, LEFKOSIA

Below: *The Archbishop's Palace, part of a large complex in the old city.*

Several of the city's museums lie inside the walls in **Kyprianos Square**. This complex of buildings includes both the new palace, built in neo-Byzantine style in 1961, and the old building it replaced. Within the palace, the **Makarios III Cultural Centre** houses an art gallery (with maps and lithographs as well as paintings), libraries and the **Byzantine Museum**, which holds the island's largest collection of icons.

The small cathedral of **Agios Ioannis**, which was built at the instigation of Archbishop Nikiforos in 1662, stands between the old and new Archbishop's palaces. Inside, its series of 18th-century frescoes depicting biblical scenes has recently been restored.

Makarios III Cultural Centre
🕐 09:00–13:00 and 14:00–17:00 Mon–Fri, 09:00–13:00 Sat
✉ Plateia Arhiepiskopou Kyprianou
☎ 22 43 00 08
📠 22 43 06 67

European Art Gallery and Byzantine Museum
🕐 Both the gallery and the museum are open 09:00–16:30 Mon–Fri and 09:00–13:00 Sat.
✉ Both are situated in the Cultural Centre.
💰 CY£1.00, or CY£0.20 for students

Below: *The Ottoman balcony of the house of Hadjigeorgakis Kornesios.*

> See Map F–C4   ★★

THE HOUSE OF HADJIGEORGAKIS KORNESIOS, LEFKOSIA

Situated roughly to the south of the Archbishop's palace (and easier to reach on foot because of a tortuous one-way system) is this fine Venetian mansion. The house is named after a resident of Térra in Pafos, who served as the official interpreter to the Turkish governor. He aided communication between the Orthodox Christians and the Ottoman authorities and held this very prestigious position between 1779 and 1809. **Hadjigeorgakis Kornesios** was one of the richest and most powerful men in Cyprus, due to the enormous wealth he accumulated through tax exemption and extensive estates. A peasant revolt was aimed at him and members of the ruling class in 1804, although he managed to find refuge and survive until he was beheaded in 1809. The mansion was built in the 15th century and has later Ottoman additions. It has been restored to house the award-winning **Cyprus Ethnographic Museum**, and its collection documents the lives of the privileged during the Ottoman period.

Hadjigeorgakis Museum
🕐 8:00–14:00 Mon–Fri, 09:00–13:00 Sat
✉ Patriarchou Grigoriou 20, Lefkosia
☎ 22 30 53 16
💰 CY£0.75

See Map E–B4 | ★★

CEDAR VALLEY

Most visitors to the Tillirian Troödos search for the Cedar Valley, advertised widely in brochures but never crowded as many give up before reaching it. It lies at the foot of Mount Tripylos, on whose slopes grow the last natural forests of indigenous cedar. The shortest route begins at Panagia, but for those with time (and determination) there are longer routes, via Lysos (southeast of Polis) or Pomos on the north coast, which are scenically rewarding.

The Cedar Valley is a unique forest. Its 200,000 indigenous cedar trees are of a species found only in Cyprus and they provide the natural habitat for the moufflon (*see* panel, page 23), a breed of large mountain goat also believed to be found exclusively in Cyprus. The moufflon are a protected species rarely seen by man outside captivity. The Cypriot Government has set up a national preserve for the breed at Stavros tis Psokas.

> **The Cyprus Cedar**
> The Cyprus Cedar is related to the Cedar of Lebanon but has much shorter needles and is considered to be unique to the island. Pit props found in ancient copper mines show that it must once have occurred throughout the Troödos. Sadly, successive invaders exploited the island's timber reserves and the cedars were inevitably a casualty. The Forestry Department has now replanted extensive areas with these trees.

Left: *The endemic Cyprus cedar* (Cedrus libani ssp. brevifolia).

⊙ *See* Map E–B4   ★★

Panagia Chrysorrogiatissa
✉ 40km (25 miles) northeast of Pafos
🕐 Open daily from morning until dusk: Apr–Sep 09:30–12:30 and 13:30–18:30; Oct–Mar 10:00–12:30 and 13:30–18:00
☎ 26 72 24 57
💰 CY£0.50

PANAGIA CHRYSORROGIATISSA

This monastery owes its Christian foundation in 1192 to the hermit **Ignatius**. One legend says he was told in a dream to build a church on the site, while another relates to the discovery of a miraculous icon (painted by St Luke). The name literally means 'Our Lady of the Golden Pomegranates' – the fruits being symbolic of, and a slang term for, breasts, it is hard to ignore a possible link with the goddess Aphrodite who is often depicted with golden breasts. The current church, built in the 1770s, stands at the head of a valley and there are dramatic views towards evening when the low sunlight emphasizes the relief of the land. The monks tend extensive vineyards below the monastery and produce and sell very palatable wines.

Agia Moni, about 2km (1 mile) from Chrysorrogiatissa, stands on the site of a temple dedicated to Hera, wife of Zeus. Abandoned in 1571, it has been renovated.

Opposite: *Where the Tillirian Troödos plunges to the sea lies Kato Pyrgos – a coast of red-brown cliffs and dark rocks.*
Right: *Panagia Chrysorrogiatissa (Our Lady of the Golden Pomegranates) is still a working monastery, producing its own wines from vineyards tended by monks in the valley below.*

See Map E–B3

★★

KATO PYRGOS

From Polis, the coast road runs northeast past extensive fruit plantations – development is beginning here but it is still a far cry from that on the south coast. **Pomos** is the largest village but it has little to commend it except for a few tavernas and some self-catering apartments. Beyond the village lies dramatic coastal scenery, where the road hugs the dark cliffs as the foothills of the Troödos tumble down into the sea.

The tortuous route through the hills circumnavigates the Turkish enclave of **Kokkina** to bring the determined driver back again to the coast road leading to Kato Pyrgos. Only UN troops can pass through the Greek and then Turkish checkpoints. Surprisingly, **Kato Pyrgos** is well-equipped with three hotels and it has an attractive beach. The Byzantine church of **Panagia Galoktisti** can be reached by walking up the valley towards Kaleri. Kato Pyrgos is about as far as you can get by road from Lefkosia, thanks to the division of the island, but for an energetic crow it is only about 60km (37 miles) away.

At several points along the coast road from Polis, signs suggest routes to Stavros tis Psokas (*see* panel, this page). Distances might not look great on a map but the innumerable bends make the journey seem endless on a hot day. One road to Stavros begins from Pomos and follows the Livadi, which is an impressive torrent in spring and winter.

Moufflon, Emblem of Cyprus
The shy and agile moufflon – used by Cyprus Airways as its logo – is seldom seen in the wild. At **Stavros** a small captive breeding herd is kept penned. The Pafos Forest is the stronghold of this wild sheep, whose exact origins are not known. Remains of these animals have been found in Neolithic settlements dating from 6000BC, at which time they may well have been domesticated. A survey in 1878 found only 20 animals. Numbers rose from 1939 when the Pafos Forest became a reserve. Both sexes grow a winter fleece of thick brown hair.

See Map E–B5 | ★★

PALEA PAFOS

Above: *La Cavocle, a Lusignan manor, dominates the much earlier site of Palea Pafos.*

The village of **Kouklia** stands on the site of Palea Pafos. Its Lusignan manor, **La Cavocle**, is visible from the main road. Much of the building dates from the Ottoman period but in Crusader days it was surrounded by sugarcane plantations. The manor is now a museum and houses finds from the adjacent site.

Little remains of ancient Pafos. The **Sanctuary of Aphrodite** comprises a hotchpotch of ruins spanning late Bronze Age to Roman times, but successive sets of local inhabitants have seen it as a convenient source of cut stone. A walk around the village reveals carved stones incorporated into the walls of the older houses. A **necropolis** is under excavation to the southeast of the hill, while on the road to **Pano Archimandrita** are remains of a siege ramp and city gate built by the Persians in 498BC.

Signposted to the south of the village is the hermitage of **Agia Pateres**. Preserved in a rock shrine here are bones, said to be those of 318 saints who were killed at Pissouri after fleeing Syria.

Sanctuary of Aphrodite
🕐 daily 09:00–17:00, but in summer (Jun–Aug) open 09:00–19:00 Mon–Fri, 09:00–17:00 Sat and Sun
✉ Kouklia Village, 14km (9 miles) east of Pafos
☎ 26 43 21 80
💰 CY£0.75

See Map E–B5   ★★

PETRA TOU ROMIOU

Petra tou Romiou is the legendary birthplace of **Aphrodite**. When the Titans hurled the severed genitalia of the unfortunate Uranus into the sea, she emerged from the resulting foam. The name, 'Rocks of Romios', derives from another legendary Cypriot, the Byzantine giant Digenis Akritas (Romios) who hurled rocks at marauding Arab pirates and kept the Byzantine Empire intact.

The coast is best seen on the journey to Pafos as the road hugs the white cliffs; for an hour or so before **sunset** the rocks are silhouetted by the scarlet globe of the sun dropping slowly to the horizon. Thanks to something as unromantic as atmospheric dust, sunsets here are spectacular, especially when, towards the end of summer, Saharan winds have whipped fine sand into the upper atmosphere and northwards towards Cyprus. A tourist pavilion stands above the road from which there are good views over the coast below. The beach is reached via a subway.

> **Aphrodite and Cyprus**
> According to the poet **Homer**, Aphrodite was the 'Cyprian' – the goddess who emerged fully grown from the foaming sea at **Petra tou Romiou** near Palea Pafos. She is also associated with a much earlier eastern deity, **Astarte**, who demanded human sacrifice and evolved into **Venus**, the Roman goddess of love. Aphrodite was also linked with battle through her support of the Trojans. However, when wounded by Diomedes, the *Iliad* records that she was reminded by a politically incorrect Zeus to 'make love, not war'. At Amathus and in other towns Aphrodite was worshiped as a bearded man, **Aphroditus**.

Left: *Lofty white cliffs form the southern coastline between Lemesos and Pafos, an appropriate setting for the legendary birth of the goddess Aphrodite at Petra tou Romiou.*

Kolossi Castle
🕐 09:00–17:00 in winter, and 09:00–19:30 in summer
✉ Kolossi; 14km (8.7 miles) west of Lemesos on the road to Pafos
☎ 25 93 49 07
💰 CY£0.75

🌐 *See* Map E–C5   ★★

KOLOSSI CASTLE, LEMESOS

The square bulk of Kolossi Castle stands to the north of Fasouri, approximately 15km (9 miles) west of Lemesos. The castle had a long association with the **Knights Hospitaller**, granted land here by Hugo I in 1210, in return for their support against the Muslims. Building started in the late 13th century on the site of Isaac Comnenos's camp.

Cyprus became the headquarters of the Order of the Knights of St John after the loss of Syria to the Arabs at Acre in 1291. The **Grand Commanderie** was established here until, in 1310, the Knights founded their own state on Rhodes, but still administered their Cyprus lands from Kolossi. The original castle was damaged during raids by the Genoese and the Mamelukes; the three-storey fortified tower, which still stands, bears the coat-of-arms of the Grand Master Louis de Magnac, dating it at around 1454.

Many villages of the south were ruled by the Knights on a feudal basis and produced olive oil, wheat, cotton, wine and sugar. A **sugar factory** with a vaulted roof stands next to the main castle: the giant millstone lies outside, close to the **aqueduct** which provided the water to power it.

The 12th-century church, **Agios Efstathios**, in the village outside the walls, was once the Knights' place of worship.

Below: *Kolossi Castle, stronghold of the Knights Hospitaller.*

⊙ See Map E–E5   ★★

CHOIROKOITIA

Below Left: *Remains of beehive-shaped houses dot the hillsides at Choirokoitia, one of the islands earliest known human settlements.*

Some of the earliest evidence of habitation on the island is found along the south coast. There are late Bronze-Age cemeteries at **Agious** and at **Agios Dimitrios** near Kalavasos, where there was a copper mine. Traces of even earlier, Stone-Age, settlements exist at **Kalavasos-Tenta** and **Choirokoitia**. The foundations of the **rotundas** at Choirokoitia were discovered in 1936, but excavations began in earnest only in 1975. The settlement dates from the 6th or 7th centuries BC

It is the site of a Neolithic settlement found in a finer state of preservation than most others from this period, not only in Cyprus but in the entire eastern Mediterranean area. It represents, through its consecutive phases of building, the whole history of the Neolithic period in Cyprus, and reveals valuable information as to the spread of the Neolithic culture throughout the region.

> **Choirokoitia**
> ⊠ 32 km (20 miles) from Larnaka town
> ☎ 24 32 27 10
> ⊕ 09:00–17:00 daily, but longer hours in summer (09:00–19:30 Mon–Fri, 09:00–17:00 Sat and Sun)
> ♿ CY£0,75

⚙ *See Map E–E4* ★★

Above: *A lacemaker demonstrates her delicate skill in Pano Lefkara, which has been famous for centuries for this distinctive craft.*

Traditional Museum of Embroidery and Silver-Smithing
⏰ 09:30–16:00 Mon–Thu and 10:00–16:00 Fri–Sat, closed on Sun.
✉ House of Patsalos, Pano Lefkara
☎ 24 34 23 26
💲 CY£0.75

PANO LEFKARA

To the east and away from the coast the land rises into the lower hills of the **Troödos** – this area is ideal for those based in Lemesos who want to explore the small country roads. The lake at **Germasogeia** is an attractive spot for a picnic.

From Kalavasos the road winds via Kellaki and the Orini region towards Melini and **Odou**; from **Choirokoitia** the same point can be reached via Vavla and Ora. Beyond Odou the vista compensates for a track which climbs dizzily in a series of sharp bends to the Troödos ridge and Pitsylia. The same route from Choirokoitia offers an alternative approach to Lefkara: via **Agios Minas** near Vavla (where the nuns sell beautiful icons, excellent honey and table grapes) to **Kato Drys**, birthplace of St Neofytos.

Of the two villages at Lefkara, the upper (**Pano Lefkara**) is the more popular because of its lacemaking (*see* panel, page 29). The restored **House of Patsalos** contains a museum of the distinctive local lacemaking and silver-smithing. Away from the centre, streets are narrow and houses have balconies and courtyards in Italianate style.

See Map E–F5 ★★

PANAGIA ANGELOKTISTOS, KITI

In **Kiti**, 11km (7 miles) from Larnaka, the original 5th-century church of Panagia Angeloktistos (meaning 'built by angels') was destroyed by Arab invaders. Most of the present building dates from the 11th and 12th centuries. The apse that remains from the earlier church, possibly from the 6th century, holds the finest mosaic to survive on Cyprus. It depicts the two Archangels, Michael and Gabriel. The church of the Virgin was built on the ruins of an earlier structure. Its present architectural form is a domed cruciform. Lazarus is said to have sailed to Kition, where he eventually died, and the original church was built over his tomb.

Cape Kiti has some beaches of indifferent quality – a mixture of sand and pebbles – though there are plenty of self-catering apartments and tavernas at **Perivolia**. There is a well-preserved **Venetian watchtower** north of the lighthouse, and another at **Alaminos**, west of Mazotos.

The Lacemakers

Lacemaking is a tradition said to have begun with the noblewomen of Lusignan and Venetian times. It is claimed that in 1481 Leonardo da Vinci bought an altarcloth made in Lefkara for Milan Cathedral. In summer, the women work outdoors in groups producing their Lefkaritika, and their menfolk sell it energetically both at home and abroad.

Panagia Angeloktistos

🕐 08:00–12:00 and 14:00–16:00 daily
✉ Kiti Village, 7km (4 miles) west of Larnaka
☎ 24 42 46 46
💰 Entry is free

Left: *Angeloktistos church in Kiti, which contains some of the finest mosaics on the island.*

See Map E–G4   ★★

Paralimni
Paralimni is quite a prosperous village, and in recent years its dependency has changed from agriculture to tourism. There are some good restaurants here (*see* page 68), and the town is a useful option for those who want to be slightly away from the throng in nearby Agia Napa.
  There are two large modern churches in Paralimni, and a small 13th-century church, **Agios Georgios**, which stands in the centre of a traffic roundabout alongside its modern counterpart. There is a salt lake to the west of the town, but it rarely fills up and then never for very long.

THE KOKKINOCHORIA

Before 1974 and the subsequent vast expansion of tourist facilities in the area, the Kokkinochoria – literally 'red soil villages' – in the southeast of the island were regarded solely as the island's eminently productive 'garden'. The rich and fertile soils, derived from weathered limestone with a high iron oxide content, are able to support up to three crops of potatoes in a single year. Unfortunately, excessive demands for water drawn from the artesian wells decreased the water table and the supply became somewhat brackish. Now a system of reservoirs (the Southern Conveyor Project) ensures uncontaminated water for all-year-round irrigation. In the villages of the hinterland, life is based around agriculture, with the villages of **Avgorou**, **Liopetri** and **Xylofagou** being lynch-pins in the island's early potato production.

From Xylofagou, early risers can make a detour to the narrow inlet at **Potamos Liopetriou**. Here, in the dawn light, you can watch small fishing boats bring their catch up the **Liopetri creek** to their anchorage at the mouth of the Liopetri River, a world away from the upmarket tourist resorts nearby.

See Map E–F4 ★★

AGIOS LAZAROS, LARNAKA

After Agios Lazaros was resurrected by Jesus, he came to Larnaka and was named the first Bishop of Kition. The Church of Agios Lazaros was built in his honour, and he still remains the local Patron of the City. The church was not 'converted' after the Ottoman conquest because in 1589 local Christians paid a heavy ransom to preserve it. But the interior is delightfully simple – the plain walls are the result of a fire in 1970.

Agia Faneromeni, to the west of Agios Lazaros, stands near a pair of rock-cut tombs. The church is reputed to have good curative powers – invoked by walking around the outside of the building three times and leaving behind an article of clothing.

The small streets in the picturesque old city of Larnaka are filled with shops, and many tavernas can be found along the seafront with its palm tree promenade.

Above: *The beautiful interior of Agios Lazaros Church.*
Opposite: *Small fishing boats bring in the daily catch up Liopetri Creek.*

Agios Lazaros
🕐 08:00–12:30 and 15:30–18:30 Mon–Sat (April–August), 08:00–12:30 and 14:30–17:00 Mon–Sat (September–March)
✉ Plateia Agiou Lazarou
☎ 24 65 24 98
♿ Entry is free

See Map J–B2 ★★

AGIA NAPA MONASTERY

Agia Napa Tourist Office
🕐 08:15–14:30 and 15:00–18:30 Mon–Fri, closed on Wed and Sat afternoons.
✉ Leoforos Kryou Nerou 12, CY 5330 Agia Napa
☎ 23 72 17 96

Right: *The monastery in Agia Napa is an unexpected haven in this busy resort.*

The Last Resort
Agia Napa is tailor-made for those in northern Europe who work hard all year and want to play hard for two weeks. For the long years when Cyprus Airways held out against charter flights from Britain, they did allow charters from Sweden, and Scandinavian workers flocked here. Young male Cypriot conscripts doing their national service longed for a posting to the camps along the coast where topless bathing had become the norm.

In spite of development the centre of Agia Napa has retained some of its charm because of the monastery, dedicated to **Our Lady of the Forests**. Built during the 16th-century Venetian period, an arched cloister encloses a courtyard with a carved octagonal **fountain** whose waters are reputed to be therapeutic. Close by are the remains of a **Roman aqueduct**, built to carry the spring water. There is also a **Folk Museum**. After the village grew in numbers, and since the monastery was no longer active, some of its rooms began to be used for the various needs of the community and especially as classrooms for the children of the elementary school. The church of the monastery became the parish church until recently when the new church was finished. The old shrine-church is still used, however, for weekday services and baptisms.

The main square outside the monastery becomes lively as evening approaches, with numerous bars, souvenir stalls and itinerant portrait painters.

See Map E–B4 ★

KYKKOS MONASTERY

Situated on a pine-covered ridge at the edge of the Tillirian Troödos, Kykkos has always played a rather prominent role in the Greek Orthodox church. It acquired immense wealth from its land in Cyprus (large areas of land in Lefkosia are owned by the church) as well as the property it once owned in mainland Greece, Asia Minor and Russia. It is the most famous and richest monastery in Cyprus. Founded in 1100 and dedicated to the Virgin Mary, it possesses one of the three surviving icons ascribed to St Luke. The valuable icon, covered in silver gilt and enclosed in a shrine of tortoiseshell and mother-of-pearl, is situated at the front of the iconostasis.

At weekends the monastery is a place of **pilgrimage**, especially for conveyor-belt baptisms of babies, and there are guest rooms available for Cypriot visitors. In EOKA (National Organization for the Cypriot Struggle) days, the monastery played an important part in sheltering the guerrillas.

Throni, a hill about 2km (1 mile) from Kykkos Monastery, is the final resting-place of **Archbishop Makarios III** who entered the monastery at the age of 12 and rose to become its Abbot, before becoming President. From the shrine on the hill above his tomb there are incredible views to Mount Olympus in the east and over the vast emptiness of the Tillirian hills in the west.

Kykkos Monastery
🕐 daily 10:00–16:00 Nov–May, 10:00–18:00 Jun–Oct
✉ 20km (12.4 miles) west of Pedoulas village
☎ 22 94 27 36
🖥 www.cyprusexplorer.com/Monasteries.htm
💰 CY£1.50 for individuals, or CY£1.00 per person for groups.

Below: *Part of the Kykkos Monastery's altar screen. The church is reputedly wealthy beyond the dreams of avarice.*

Above: *The oldest frescoes of Agia Paraskevi, in the centre of Geroskipou, date from the 9th century.*

Troödos Churches

The churches on UNESCO's list represent the cream: Asinou, Agios Ioannis Lampadistis, Agios Nikolaos tis Stegis, Panagia tou Araka and Stavros tou Agiasmati. Occasionally, you may turn up 'on spec' to find the church already open for other visitors, but don't rely on it. To find the caretaker, ask at the nearest village café. Don't expect a guided tour with a discussion of the finer points of Byzantine art. There are no admission charges, but a suitable donation is CY£1.00.

Places of Worship

Agia Paraskevi

The church, southeast of Pafos in Geroskipou, is unique in having five tiled domes. Decorations over its altar date from the 9th century, while the earliest fresco dates from the 10th century.
⊠ *Geroskipou village, Pafos;* ☎ *26 96 18 59;* ⏱ *Apr–Oct: 08:00–13:00 and 14:00–17:00 Mon–Sat; Nov–Mar: 08:00–13:00 and 14:00–16:00 Mon–Sat (25–26 July marks the feast of the patron saint).*

Agios Andronikos

This Byzantine church was taken over by the Ottoman Turks and used as a mosque until the evacuation of the Turkish Cypriot population. Since then, the 16th-century frescoes have been painstakingly cleaned by archaeologists from the Department of Antiquities.
⊠ *Polis Chrysochous, 17km (10 miles) north of Pafos.*

Machairas Monastery

Situated in Troödos, the monastery's foundation in 1148 began in time-honoured fashion with the discovery of a miraculous icon (painted by St Luke) by two hermits from Palestine. Funds were provided for the construction by the Emperor Comnenos. The monastery twice had to be rebuilt after a fire – once in 1530 and again in 1892.
⊠ *41km (25 miles) south of Lefkosia through Deftera and Pera villages;* ⏱ *09:00–12:00 Mon, Tue and Thu.*

Stavrovouni Monastery

Women are prohibited from entering this monastery in the western Larnaka district, even though its foundation is attributed to a female, Empress Helena, mother of Constantine the Great, who left a splinter of the 'true cross' here when she was shipwrecked in AD327. It is claimed that this fragment, encased in silver and set in another cross, survived the destruction of the monastery by Arabs in 1426 and by Turks in 1570. The monastery was rebuilt in the 1800s and today a small group of monks leads a rigorous life of work and prayer here.

✉ 9km (5.5 miles) off the Lefkosia-Lemesos Road, 40km (25 miles) from Larnaka;
🕐 08:00–12:00 and 14.00–17.00 Sep–Mar, 08:00–12:00 and 15:00–18:00 Apr–Aug.

Agios Irakleidios

This old monastery in Machairas was destroyed and rebuilt several times since it was founded in the 4th century. It was taken over by nuns in 1963. Those in the know get their pot plants here; also on sale are honey and kapari (capers).

✉ Politiko village, 0,5 km from the Royal Tombs.

Asinou Church

The finest of all the painted churches on the island, this church in Solea – the northern region of Troödos – dates from 1105. The dome and narthex were added in 1200 and the frescoes are a catalogue of Byzantine art. Five layers of paintings span the period from the building of the church to the 16th century.

✉ Adelfi Forest;
☎ 22 85 29 22;
🕐 09:00–17:00 in summer; 09:00–16:00 in winter.

Agios Nikolaos tis Stegis

The name of the church, 'St Nicholas of the Roof', refers to its large pitched roof. This church, also in Solea, contains many frescoes dating from the 11th to the 17th centuries; the *Nativity* is very impressive.

✉ 5 km from Kakopetria village;
🕐 09:00–16:00 Tue–Sat, 11:00–16:00 Sun.

Afxentiou's Tomb

Below the monastery of Machairas, a path leads to the cave where Gregor Afxentiou, a prominent EOKA member (who had been sheltered by the monks) was eventually cornered. His colleagues surrendered but he did not – although wounded, he determinedly held off a platoon of 60 British troops for ten hours. He was eventually killed by a petrol bomb thrown into the cave.

Below: *The monastery of Machairas has twice had to be rebuilt as a result of fires.*

Mosaic Design

The best mosaics were formed from cubes of coloured glass (*tesserae*), sometimes with gold leaf applied; others employed cubes of coloured stone. Pre-Christian mosaics depict scenes taken from tales of the Greek gods and heroes. Later compositions were laid over the earlier versions, with the influence of Christianity showing up in geometric designs and floral motifs. In general, human figures are shown full-face, but animals, pagans and the wicked appear in profile. Originally, mosaics were kept highly polished and were a lot brighter.

Below: *The Phoenician tombs in Pafos were never the last resting place of royalty, but their sheer scale has led to their being called the Tombs of the Kings.*

Historic Sites
The Mosaics

Pafos is famed for its floor mosaics from the 2nd and 3rd centuries AD in houses named after the characters depicted: the House of Dionysos, the House of Orpheus, the House of the Four Seasons, the House of Aion and the House of Theseus.

✉ *Kyriakou Nikolaou, Kato Pafos;*
☎ *26 94 02 17;*
💰 *CY£1.50;*
🕐 *08:00–17:00 daily, but 08:00–19:30 daily in summer.*

The Odeion

North of the mosaics, near the lighthouse, this small, 2nd-century Roman theatre was damaged by an earthquake and abandoned in the 7th century.

Partly restored, it is connected by a corridor to the **Asklepeion** (centre of healing); nearby lie the bases of Corinthian columns showing the position of the **agora** (marketplace). The remains of a Hellenistic altar comprise foundations and a set of steps.

✉ *Kato Pafos;*
🕐 *Permanently open.*

The Tombs of the Kings

Dating from the Ptolemaic period, the tombs lie off the road north of Pafos to Coral Bay. No royalty was actually buried here, but with about 100 tombs on the headland, the site's scale is impressive. Behind a façade of Doric columns, the tombs are cut out of rock – some are particularly grand.

✉ *2km (1.2 miles) north of Kato Pafos;*
☎ *26 30 26 95;*
💰 *CY£0.75;* 🕐 *daily 08:00–17:00 Nov–Mar, 08:00–18:00 Apr–May and Sep–Oct, 08:00–19:30 Jun–Aug.*

Tamassos

Tamassos, occupied since 2500BC, was long famed as a centre of copper mining and export. By 800BC, it was a Phoenician colony, but later mine owners included Alexander the Great and King Herod. In 1874, several tombs were excavated, possibly belonging to kings of Tamassos.

⌧ *Politiko village, 20km (12 miles) south-west of Lefkosia;*

⦿ *CY£0.75;*

⊕ *The site is open 09:00–15:00 Tue–Fri, 10:00–15:00 Sat–Sun, and closed Mon.*

Amathus

The site of the ancient city kingdom of Amathus lies just north of the main coastal road of Lemesos. Uncovered so far are the remains of a huge agora, a Christian basilica, an extensive sluice system and numerous houses, but the probable extent of what still lies hidden down to the coast is vast. During the construction of the Amathus Beach Hotel, tombs were discovered and there are remains of harbour walls under the sea.

⌧ *11km (7 miles) east of Lemesos;*

⦿ *CY£0.75;*

⊕ *09:00–17:00 daily, but 09:00–19:30 daily in summer.*

Kition

Much of the ancient city kingdom of Kition lies beneath modern Larnaka. The remains found here date from a number of distinctly different periods: there is one site where there was once an acropolis, a Mycenaean site, part of a Mycenaean city built on top of an earlier 1300BC settlement, and remains of a later Phoenician settlement.

⌧ *500m north of the Archaeological Museum;*

⦿ *CY£0.75;*

⊕ *09:00–14:30 Mon–Fri, 15:00–17:00 Thu.*

Above: *The ancient Odeion and light-house at Pafos.*

Catacombs

The soft sandstone around and below **Fabrica Hill** is honey-combed with carved tunnels, chambers and tombs. Several have been used as shrines since the time of the early Christians. When and by whom the chambers were hollowed is not known, since they predate Christian worship. Two catacombs are dedicated to recognized Cypriot saints **Solomóni** and **Lambrianós**, but others suggest a pagan devotion to dubious 'saints' **Agapitikos** and **Misitikos**, representing love (*agapi*) and hate (*misos*) respectively. All the catacombs are reputed to have magical properties.

Above: *The Pierides Foundation Museum in Larnaka houses artefacts from all over Cyprus.*

Apollo's Head
In 1836, a bronze statue of Apollo, cast in Athens in the 5th century, was discovered on the site of **Tamassos** by local farmers. Unfortunately, they broke it up and sold the valuable bronze to a scrap metal merchant. The head alone was salvaged and now resides in the British Museum.

Museums
The Houses of Achilleas Dimitri and Katsinioros
Traditional hill villages in Machairas exhibit rural architecture, using bricks of sun-baked mud or dung mixed with straw, and with tiled roofs. Fikardou has been rescued from disrepair by the Museum Service, which is restoring the buildings. The houses of Achilleas Demitri and Katsinioros date from the 16th century and contain typical traditional furniture and implements.
⊠ *Fikardou;* ☎ *22 63 47 31;* 👗 *CY£0.75;* ⊕ *Sep–May: 09:00– 16:00 Tue–Fri, 09:00– 15:30 Sat, 10:30–14:30 Sun; Jun–Aug: 09:30– 16:30 Tue–Fri, 09:30– 16:00 Sat.*

Cyprus Medieval Museum, Lemesos
The collection here includes part of the Lambousa treasure from AD620, found near Keryneia, and also some sets of Lusignan armour.
⊠ *The Citadel, Lemesos;* ☎ *25 33 04 19;* 👗 *CY£1.00;* ⊕ *09:00–17:00 Mon– Sat, 10:00–13:00 Sun.*

Archaeological Museum, Lemesos
The District Archaeological Museum is housed in a modern building in

Lemesos. It displays collections of finds from Amathus, Kourion and elsewhere. Room 1 concentrates on the Neolithic period, Room 2 on jewellery and pottery, and Room 3 on sculptures, of which those from Amathus reveal Egyptian as well as Greek influences.

✉ corner of Vyronos and Kaningos streets, Lemesos;

☎ 25 30 51 57;

💰 CY£0.75;

🕐 09:00–17:00 Mon–Fri, 10:00–13:00 Sat.

The Pierides Foundation Museum, Larnaka

Demetrios Pierides, a Cypriot scholar, founded this museum of antiquities in Larnaka in 1839. Unlike other local museums, it shows artefacts from all over the island, many saved from tomb robbers by its wealthy founder. The collection is housed in an 18th-century town-house and exhibits range from Neolithic pottery, through Archaic and Classical terracotta figures to Byzantine glass.

✉ 4 Zinonos Kitieos;

☎ 24 81 45 55;

💰 CY£1.00; 🕐 09:00–16:00 Mon–Thu, 09:00–13:00 Fri–Sat.

Cyprus Archaeological Museum, Lefkosia

Outside the walls near the Pafos Gate, the large cool building of the Cyprus Museum houses, within its 14 rooms, the finest discoveries from sites all over the island. Here is arguably the best archaeological collection in the Middle East, spanning over 7000 years of history from Neolithic times (6800BC) to the early Byzantine period.

✉ 1 Leoforos Mouseiou;

☎ 22 86 58 88;

💰 CY£1.50;

🕐 09:00–17:00 Mon–Sat, 10:00–13:00 Sun and public holidays.

The First Cypriots

Discoveries from Choirokoitia, now in the Cyprus Museum in Lefkosia, show that the inhabitants were mainly farmers. **Obsidian** artefacts indicate that they traded with Asia Minor, since the volcanic rock obsidian does not occur in Cyprus. These early Cypriots – the **Eteo-Cypriots** – worshipped a mother goddess and buried their dead either beneath the floors of their homes or just outside. Infant mortality was high, judging by the number of small skeletons found.

Below: The Cyprus Museum in Lefkosia boasts a magnificent archaeological collection.

Below: *The evocatively named baths of Aphrodite.*

National Parks
Akamas

Proposed as the island's first National Park in 1989, Akamas is situated at the westernmost part of Cyprus. It embraces a total of some 155km² (60 sq miles), encompassing a varied terrain with beaches, cliffs, gorges and forests, as well as a number of picturesque villages. The region's main feature is a rugged peninsula ending in Cape Arnaoutis (Cape Akamas), with the tiny islet of Mazaki beyond it.

Troödos Forest

Troödos National Forest Park is situated in the center of the island and covers an area of 9337ha (23,072 acres). The area is simply magical and is suitable for hiking, skiing (during winter), mountain biking, nature study and picnics. The thick cedar and pine forests and sun-soaked slopes of the Troödos region offer an unexpected contrast to the Mediterranean coast. Signs mark the presence of flora and fauna unique to Cyprus.

ACTIVITIES
Sport and Recreation

Local sporting passions are directed largely towards **football** and **tennis**. Resorts in the south cater for a variety of **water sports**, from swimming and scuba diving to windsurfing and parascending. Contact the **Cyprus Federation of Underwater Activities** in Lefkosia, ☎ 22 75 46 47, 📠 22 75 52 46.

There are plenty of opportunities to watch or participate in **tennis**, with numerous private clubs and hotel courts. **Hiking** is being promoted by the CTO, given the vast network of mountain trails and reasonably predictable weather in spring and autumn. The northern hills are ideal for hikers, but involve dodging the rather ubiquitous military camps.

Mountain biking is becoming popular in Cyprus – for more information, *see* page 48. The **Cyprus Motor Rally** (*see* panel, this page) also attracts a lot of interest, both local and international – especially since points are gained for the European Championship.

In winter, the Troödos offers **skiing**: three lifts on the northeastern face of Mount Olympus are open from late December to March or early April. **Golfers** will find an 18-hole, par 72 golf course near Pafos and Lemesos.

Horse-riding centres are scattered throughout the island, and an annual **kite-flying** festival takes place in the first week of March, organized by the Pafos municipality.

> **The Cyprus Rally**
> Held each year in September, the Cyprus Rally attracts both locally based and well-known international competitors to an event with increasing prestige and great national support.
> The race begins in Lefkosia and moves quickly onto the winding roads and tracks of the Troödos mountains. Every stage is very well planned and marked so that the non-racing driver has no risk of getting caught up in a nightmare.

Below: *Skiing in Cyprus is for fun rather than for serious enthusiasts.*

Above: *Olive trees are a very familiar feature of the Cyprus countryside.*

Hidden Cyprus

Many of the people who visit Cyprus do not stray much further than the beaches and the coastal strip. But this island is the one place where it really is worth hiring a car and exploring inland; a completely different world awaits you here. There are a number of marked **hiking trails** going right across the Troödos Mountains, where the only sound you will hear is the wind in the pine trees and the splashing of a mountain stream. And just a few miles into the hills behind Lemesos and Pafos are tiny **villages**, where old men still ride donkeys and the village taverna is the hub of social life. Fikardou, Omodos, Lefkara and Kakopetria are all worth seeking out.

Realizing that visitors were hungry to see the 'real' Cyprus, the CTO recently established the **Cyprus Association of Agrotourism**, a body promoting holidays in the Cyprus countryside. Local people have been encouraged to restore traditional houses to create rural tourist accommodation, and the result is an enticing collection of 51 beautiful, traditional houses and villas in pretty villages, many of them worthy of a place in a glossy style magazine. The association also details the best villages to explore, pointing visitors towards some of the lesser-known sights, tiny museums and the best views.

Cyprus Agrotourism Company
⊠ Leoforos Lemesou 19, PO Box 24535, CY 1390 Lefkosia
☎ 22 33 77 15
📠 22 33 97 23
🖥 www.agrotourism.com.cy
🖥 www.yourcyprus.com/agrotourism/

Fun for Children

Cyprus is an excellent destination for those travelling with children. As is the case in most Mediterranean countries, children are always made welcome in restaurants and bars. Most of the **beaches** have blue flags, and hotels and apartments have a wide variety of facilities and activities that are safe for children. An overwhelming majority of **hotels** host special children's entertainment. Furthermore, many hotels make special arrangements offering free child accommodation or a discount for children, and even babysitting facilities.

Hotels in Cyprus with particularly good facilities for children include Le Meridien in Lemesos, which has a self-contained children's club; the Coral Beach near Pafos – a large hotel built in traditional style with a wide range of facilities and a children's club; and the deluxe Anassa at Polis, one of the island's most beautiful and expensive hotels, situated on a deserted sandy beach.

Pafos is a family resort – it is peaceful and has plenty of activities for children. Protaras also has much to offer families with children. Beaches around the southeast corner of the island are very good, with the fine white sand sought after by holiday-makers – in summer the beaches around Agia Napa get very crowded and should probably be avoided by those seeking peace and quiet. A wide range of water sports, anything from pedaloes to parascending, is also available.

> **Reptile Exhibit**
> Don't miss the well-housed exhibition on the **Reptiles of Cyprus** set up at Skoulli, south of Polis on the main road to Pafos. Its intention is to interest and educate both visitors and locals, who view things which slither and crawl with loathing. Only one snake, the blunt-nose viper, poses any danger to humans.

Below: The beaches of Cyprus are an excellent playground for children.

Akamas Nature Trails
The **Baths of Aphrodite** are the starting point for several nature trails. The CTO and the Cyprus Forestry Department have taken a lot of trouble to waymark paths on Akamas. Along the trails some of the plants are labelled with Greek (and Latin) numbers corresponding to leaflets which are available from the tourist office; they also provide a very good free map of the area on a scale of 1:100,000.

Walking Tours
Exploring Akamas

The mountains along the peninsular spine end in a 'table top' rising to **Mavri Schinia** at 480m (1575ft), which can be reached wholly on foot by the energetic via a well-marked trail from **Loutra Aphroditis**. Views are stupendous: the land drops away in precipitous cliffs over tiny bays and inlets set in an azure sea. Alternatively, the heights can be gained via the village of **Neo Chorio**, where rooms are available for rent. A dirt road beyond the village leads to a roadside spring at **Smigies** and the tiny chapel of **Agios Minas**. Where the open pinewoods begin, there is a picnic place complete with tables and cooking areas. Beyond, the dirt road divides – the left fork is negotiable by four-wheel drive, slowly and carefully! The descent via hairpin bends offers breathtaking vistas of the sea, and the road eventually reaches Lara Beach. The right fork leads to a forest road winding along the ridge to **Kefalovrisia** and an ancient site, **Kastroiotis Rigaenas**, where another picnic spot has been set up near a spring running beneath the shade of huge oak trees (often a feature of Lusignan settlements). In summer, try to make the final climb to the exposed heights in the early morning or evening, when the air is cooler and clearer.

Below: *One of the last wild places on the island, Akamas is equally attractive to both conservationists and developers – only time will tell who wins.*

44

The Avagas Gorge
From the coastal road beyond **Agios Georgios**, north of Pafos, tracks climb through a landscape of spectacular valleys cut by rivers flowing to the sea. Although parts of the route may be negotiable by four-wheel drive vehicles, the only

Above: *Along the lonely coast north of Coral Bay, the sea has sculpted the soft white chalk into an unusual landscape of arches and columns.*

way to appreciate this unspoiled part of the island is on foot. In summer, a sun hat and a supply of water is essential; in spring and autumn walking is comfortable and the chance of meeting anyone else is very remote. The Avagas Gorge (from *avga*, meaning eggs, supposedly collected from the cliffs for food) has a special allure – the sculpted rock walls close in on a valley seldom penetrated by the sun's rays. It is a scramble (two hours plus) up through the gorge to **Kato Arodes**; alternatively, a downhill trek can be started here.

You will need a good map (free from the tourist board) to find the exact starting point of the gorge, which almost falls away from the rocky coastal plain. Deep inside, the limestone walls tower 30m (98ft) overhead, and a cool, silent river flows slowly along the floor. Snakes and other reptiles as well as ferns can be found down here. If you are lucky, you will have the gorge to yourself. Certain areas require a bit of scrambling; this is not a hike suitable for anybody of limited mobility.

Avagas Gorge
Location: Map E–A4
Duration: 30–40 minutes
Start and Finish: Avagas Gorge
🍽 Viklari
☎ 26 99 60 88

Above: *Remains of ancient aqueduct systems occur in the Xeros and other valleys.*

Horteri Trail
Location: Map L–B1
Distance: 5km (3 miles)
Duration: 2 hours
Start and finish:
Stavros tis Psokas forest station
Route: Circular hike around eastern side of Stavros Valley.

Selladi tou Stavrou
Location: Map L–B1
Distance: 2.6km (1.6 miles)
Start and finish:
Stavros tis Psokas forest station
Route: Circular hike around northern side of Stavros Valley.

Tilliria

Once famed for its copper deposits, Tilliria is a vast area of wooded conical peaks to the east of the Polis–Pafos road. This wild area falls within the **Pafos Forest** and an extensive network of well-maintained forest roads offers endless opportunities for those who need to escape the crowds. With care, four-wheel drive is not essential.

East of Koilineia, the road deteriorates to a track at Vretsia and then descends to the upper end of the **Xeros Valley**. Here, the **Roudia Bridge**, now restored, formed part of the **Venetian camel route** established to carry copper ore from mines on the heights of Troödos to the sea coast at Pafos. In spring and early summer there is still an appreciable amount of water in the Xeros, though in midsummer it lives up to its name (*xeros* means dry).

The geology of the area is remarkable – the road back to Pafos down the Diarizos Valley passes a succession of different coloured rocky outcrops, where upheavals in the earth's crust have revealed long-hidden strata. The Turkish village of **Mamonia** has given its name to a series of ancient fossil-bearing rocks, the Mamonia Complex.

The Xeros Valley can also be reached from Agios Nikolaos (in Troödos) – the road is 'jeepable', but it is almost an insult to this unspoiled area to attempt to explore it any other way than on foot. Walking offers your best chance of seeing Egyptian vultures soaring high over the terrain from the inaccessible cliffs on which they nest. The Kelefos Bridge is approached via a track running north from Agios Nikolaos.

The Madari Ridge

In spring and autumn Pitsylia, in Troödos, offers a great deal to the walker. The **Madari Ridge nature trail** meanders across a high, wooded ridge with commanding views on either side. There are two trails, which can be combined to make a three and a half hour hike. The first starts at Doxasi o Theos (Glory to God), 2km (1.2 miles) from Kyperounta and 5km (3 miles) from Spilia. The trail through the pine-scented forest leads to the Mandari fire lookout at over 1600m (5250ft), with tantalizing views of the distant Mediterranean glinting in the sun. From the end of this trail, follow the Teisa tis Madaris route for 3km (2 miles) around Madaris peak for more breathtaking views from the towering cliffs. This is a relatively easy walk, some of it on tarmac road, but be sure to take plenty of water as there is nowhere to buy refreshments up here.

Pitsylia has a few special attractions for botanists in spring, when some of the island's rarest bulbous plants flower, albeit briefly and well away from prying eyes. **Hartmann's Crocus** and the delicate blue **Lady Lock's Chionodoxa** are two of the finest examples. Apples, pears, cherries, peaches and grapes are grown in the region too.

The Madari Ridge
Location: Map K–F2
Distance: 3.75km (2.3 miles)
Duration: 2 hours
Start: Doxasi o Theos
Finish: Mandari fire lookout

Teisa tis Madaris
Location: Map E–C4
Distance: 3km (2 miles)
Duration: 1½ hours
Start and finish: Teisa tis Madaris

Below: *Lady Lock's chionodoxa (Chionodoxa Lochiae) is one of the island's rarest plants.*

Below: *A solitary church in a wild area of small vine-yards and scrub-covered hills south of Polis.*

Organized Tours
Pafos and the West

All travel agents offer **coach tours** of the area (details are posted in most hotel foyers). **Boat trips** are available from Pafos harbour (including a glass-bottomed boat), Lakki and Coral Bay (Agios Georgios). Numerous 'safari' operators offer **treks**, but some are more interested in picnics than wildlife – try **Exalt**, ✉ 35 Georgios A, Potmasos Germasoigas, Lemesos, ☎ 25 31 51 45.

Troödos

Full-day and half-day coach trips visit the Troödos region – especially the hill resorts – from the main tourist centres on the coast.

The only **organized tours** in the Troödos area which include walking and hiking are offered by **Exalt** (*see* above).

Various well-planned and highly scenic **mountain bike routes**, graded from novice to difficult, are offered by the **Jubilee Mountain Bike Centre**, ✉ Jubilee Hotel, Troödos, ☎ 25 42 15 47, 🖷 25 46 39 91. Mountain bikes can be hired on a daily or a weekly basis, and at very reasonable rates.

Lemesos

The main tour operators offer a pick-up service from the Lemesos hotels, with both day and overnight excursions all over the island. Several operators offer 3-day cruises to **Egypt** and even

Lebanon – these are widely advertised in all the hotels and at travel agents. These tours represent excellent value for money as a 'holiday from a holiday'. In times of peace in the Middle East, the cruises also operate to Israel.

If you're interested in **wine**, there's a daily KEO tour (see panel, page 65) of the Commandaria cellars in Franklin Roosevelt at 10:00, ☎ 25 36 20 53. Booking is essential in summer, but at other times of the year it would be sufficient to arrive in the reception area of the administration building.

Larnaka

The main tour operators offer a pick-up service from all hotels, with day and overnight excursions all over the island.

Lefkosia

Most of the main tour operators here also offer a pick-up service from all the Lefkosia hotels, with day and overnight excursions all over the island.

Organized walking tours of the city start from the CTO in Laïki Geitonia; check with them for details of routes and times.

Above: *Dividing north from south, the Green Line has only one crossing for day visitors near the old Ledra Palace Hotel in Lefkosia.*

Above: *Shopping in Onasagoras Street, Lefkosia: there are few real bargains, but plenty to grab the attention.*

<u>**Shopping**</u>
Although much of greater Lefkosia is modern and a brash testament to the use of concrete in terms of its architecture, shopaholics will find plenty of diversion along Makarios III Avenue and the adjoining streets. Within the walls good buys, including leather bags, jackets and shoes, can be found along the bustling thoroughfares of Odos Lidras and Onasagoras. Designer spectacles cost half as much as elsewhere in Europe – bring your prescription or take a new test – and will be ready in 24 hours.

Shops

For a directory of shops in Cyprus, visit 🖳 *www.directory. welcometocyprus.com/ shopping*

Fior

A wide range of leather goods, such as <u>shoes and handbags.</u>
☎ *22 75 12 22,* ✆ *cynav@cytanet.com.cy*

Christina's

Considered by some to be one of the most beautiful shops on the island, take time to visit Christina's in Pissouri. Contained in three large rooms, you can see a marvellous selection of Cypriot art and crafts, plus a wide range of gifts, flowers, glassware, and pottery.
☎ *25 22 20 48,*
✆ *25 22 27 17,*
✆ *davit@ cytanet.com.cy*
🖳 *www.christinas-gallery-pissouri.com*

Margarita

Sells a large range of jewellery, souvenirs and gifts.

✉ *4 Eleftherias Street, Agia Napa,*
☎ *23 72 16 65.*

House of Crafts

View the work of up to thirty local artists and craft workers, displayed in the unique setting of a stenciled old Cypriot house. Five rooms are overflowing with tasteful, good-quality handicrafts, ideal for gifts, keepsakes and interior <u>design/decoration.</u>
✉ *100 Arch. Kyprianou Avenue (opposite the Chrysopolitissa Church), 6015 Larnaka*
☎ *24 66 47 60,*
✆ *24 66 47 60,*
✆ *info@ houseofcraftscy.com*

George Kotsonis

This shop has a good selection of paintings and silkcreens by the well-known artist <u>George Kotsonis.</u>
✉ *27 Eleftheriou Venizelou Avenue, Pafos,* ☎ *26 93 27 02,*
✆ *24 66 47 60,*
✆ *info@ kotsoniscy.com*

SHOPS

Apocalypse Gallery

The gallery exhibits a completely new collection of various art forms every three weeks. The art forms on display may include paintings, sculptures and several other types of art.

✉ 30 Chytron, Tofarco House, Lefkosia,
☎ 22 76 66 55,
📠 22 76 55 90.

CNA Pottery

This is where you can find a wide variety of traditional ceramic arts. You will also have the opportunity to watch the whole process of pottery making, from the first steps right up to the finished product.

✉ Leoforos Chlorakas, PO Box 60731, Pafos,
☎ 99 45 67 50,
📠 26 45 67 50.

S.D. Lady Boutique

This boutique sells a selection of beautifully crafted clothes, imported from France, Italy and Spain.

✉ Zenonos Kitieos Street, Shop 5, Larnaka
☎ 24 65 07 69,
📠 24 65 07 69.

Mini Shops

Top quality leather goods are available here, as well as a good selection of reasonably priced handicrafts and souvenirs.

✉ 8 Anexartisias Street, and 49A St Andrews Street, Lemesos,
☎ 25 37 98 60.

A.Z. Orthodox Byzantine Icons Centre Ltd

Here you can find hand-painted icons made by monks in the monasteries, including some by specialized icon painters. If you have special orders and requests, a period of three weeks' notice must be given.

✉ 26A Anexartisias Street, CY-3036, Lemesos,
☎ 25 34 12 95 or 25 34 12 97,
📠 25 34 13 06.

Cyprus Handicraft Service Shops
Lefkosia:
✉ 186 Athalassa Avenue;
☎ 22 30 50 24

Larnaka:
✉ 6 Cosma Lysioti;
☎ 24 63 03 27

Lemesos:
✉ 25 Thermidos;
☎ 25 30 51 18

Pafos:
✉ 64 Apostolos Pavlos Avenue;
☎ 26 24 02 43.

Foini Furniture
Foini chairs and stools are famous throughout Cyprus. Once, but no longer, manufactured by **Philippos Kallis,** they are beautifully turned, with legs and arms made from carefully selected branches of the strawberry tree (*Arbutus*), with stringers of Cyprus oak and woven seats.

Ceramics
Kornos, off junction 11 on the motorway, is a ceramics centre selling ornamental troughs, garden pots and huge storage vessels called *pithari*. Prices are good, but the difficulty of getting goods home by air is offputting. For those who settle in Cyprus, this is the place to come to stock a patio. There is also a pottery centre at **Kofinou** to the south.

Below: *Town markets offer an unbeatable source of fruit, vegetables and general provisions for self-caterers, and often sell good locally made crafts rather than tourist 'tat'.*

Markets
Ktima Covered Market

Be sure not to miss the covered market in Ktima. It is a good place to buy various locally produced wares such as lace, tablecloths, bed linen and leather items. Here you will find meat, fish, and a good selection of fresh fruit and vegetables. Also on sale are Cyprus Delights, a tasty sweet that is made locally. There are several restaurants and cafés in the area, so a variety of refreshment is available.

✉ *Makariou III Street, Ktima.*

Polis Market

Don't miss the wonderful municipal covered market in the centre of the small town of Polis. It is still geared to the needs of the locals, and is a very good source of cheap fruit and vegetables of excellent quality. It is an especially good place to shop for produce if you intend cooking for yourself during your stay here.

✉ *Plateia Iroon (main square), central Polis.*

Larnaka City Covered Market

Among the usual run of ordinary market stalls, you can also find fine copper and silver goods on sale at this market.

⊠ *At the southern end of Zinonos Kitios, Larnaka.*

Lefkosia Municipal Market

A variety of fresh fruit and vegetables is brought to this market by the most amazing collection of village buses.

⊠ *Just off Trikoupi Road, in Lefkosia's Old Town.*

Laïki Geitonia, Lefkosia

While not strictly a market, this is one of the prettiest and most interesting districts of Lefkosia. The houses here have been beautifully restored, and a lot of them are used as craftsmen's workshops and art galleries. These are interspersed with restaurants, many with a shady, vine-covered terrace, a welcome respite from the soaring temperatures Lefkosia can endure in the summer months. These restaurants often serve much better food than the tourist traps on the coast.

⊠ *Situated in the pedestrian area within the walled city of Old Lefkosia.*

Lefkara

This sleepy little village is the heart of the island's lace-making industry (*see also page 28*), much of which comes from the cottage industries. Old women and young girls alike turn out the most beautifully intricate pieces of lace which they use for making tablecloths, shawls and napkins. These are usually sold at better prices than those offered by the souvenir shops in the tourist resorts.

⊠ *Inland from Lemesos.*

A Feast of Cherries

The valleys of the lower Troödos provide ideal conditions for fruit growing: apricots, apples, peaches and especially cherries. In spring, the hillsides become drifts of blossom, and around Whitsun (the eighth week after Easter), roadside stalls offer mountains of black cherries – an appropriate measure is the oke (about 1.5kg or 3lb) which might seem greedy, but only to those who have never tried them. Later in the year, fragrant dried cherries are a delicious local speciality.

Cyprus Handicrafts

For gifts with a Cypriot flavour take a taxi to the **Cyprus Handicrafts Centre** on Athalassa Avenue (turn right at the lights at the beginning of the Lefkosia–Lemesos highway). In workshops set around a quiet courtyard, are weavers, potters and woodcarvers, all displaced from the north. The centre has outlets in **Laïki Geitonia** and in all the major towns.

Above: *Hotels large and small, and tourism in general, have greatly contributed to the meteoric recovery in the Cypriot economy and to an enviably high standard of living for its inhabitants.*

The Package Trade

A very large proportion of visitors to Cyprus book all-inclusive holidays, making it almost impossible for the independent traveller to arrive in summer and find accommodation 'on spec'. In the five winter months the situation is a lot less difficult, although the number of visitors arriving at this time of year is increasing.

WHERE TO STAY

From June to early September most hotels are geared to the pre-booked **package trade** – look for last-minute bargains from your travel agent. The CTO provides free brochures, listing hotels, apartments and other accommodation. **Prices** are government-controlled according to category and, by law, rates must be displayed in hotel rooms. Outside the main season and major holidays such as Easter, finding accommodation 'on spec' poses few problems: CTO offices can help. Pensions are few and far between, except in the northwest (Polis). **English** is spoken in all hotels.

Camping is officially permitted only at licensed campsites, though a flexible attitude is adopted by locals and visitors alike. There are six sites, five of which are on the coast.

Youth hostels exist in all the main centres: Lefkosia, ☎ 22 44 48 08, Lemesos, ☎ 25 36 37 49, Larnaka, ☎ 24 62 15 08, Pafos, ☎ 26 23 25 88 and in two forest areas: Troödos, ☎ 25 42 16 49, and at the forest station, Stavros tis Psokas, ☎ 26 72 23 38. An International Youth Hostel card is needed.

Pafos
• *LUXURY*
Annabelle
(Map A–B3)
Good views over the harbour from its lush gardens; every facility is available.
⊠ Poseidonis,
☎ 26 23 83 33,
📠 26 24 55 02,
📧 the-annabelle@ thanos.hotels.com.cy
🖥 www.thanoshotels. com

• *MID-RANGE*
Dionysos (Map A–B3)
Efficient, friendly and comfortable, with a great bar tastefully built to look like the antiquities of Pafos.
⊠ PO Box 60141,
1 Dionysos Street,
☎ 26 93 34 14, 📠 26 93 39 08, 📧 dionysos@ spidernet.com.cy
🖥 www.dionysos-hotels/paphos.com

Axiothea (Map A–B1)
Friendly, reliable and well run, with good view over Nea Pafos.
⊠ PO Box 60070,
2 Ivi Malioti Street,
☎ 26 23 28 66,
📠 26 24 57 90.

Park Mansion
(Map E–A5)
This delightful Venetian-style mansion has a swimming pool.
⊠ 16 Odos Pavlou Melas, Ktima, ☎ 26 24 56 45, 📠 26 24 64 15.

Coral Bay
• *LUXURY*
Leptos Coral Beach
(Map E–A4)
Luxury resort with beach, spa, swimming pools and children's facilities.
⊠ Pegeia, Coral Bay,
☎ 26 88 10 00,
📠 26 66 29 30.
📧 manager@ coral.com.cy
🖥 www.leptos-hotels.com

Polis
• *MID-RANGE*
Droushia Heights
(Map E–A4)
Fine views of Polis, Tilliria and Akamas. Staff are friendly and efficient, and rooms comfortable.
⊠ Drouseia 8700, PO Box 66130, 8830 Polis,
☎ 26 33 23 51, 📠 26 33 23 53.

Marion (Map E–A4)
This establishment is clean, comfortable and almost legendary for its service at languid 'Polis' speed.
⊠ PO Box 66029,
☎ 26 32 14 59,
📠 26 32 21 24.

• *BUDGET*
Akamas (Map E–A4)
Very basic accommodation but not run-of-the-mill. Front rooms get some traffic noise.
⊠ PO Box 66205,
☎ 26 32 15 21,
📠 26 32 15 61.

Troödos
• *MID-RANGE*
Jubilee (Map K–C2)
One-of-a-kind hotel based around a series of chalets; comfortable and unpretentious with good food. Convenient for walking. Activity holidays for children in summer; good centre for skiers in winter with roaring fires.
⊠ PO Box 21250,
1504, Lefkosia,
☎ 25 42 01 07, 📠 22 67 39 91, 🖥 www. jubileehotel.com

Platres

• *LUXURY*

Forest Park

(Map K–C3)

Well-appointed luxury hotel surounded by scented pine forests.
✉ 62 Sp. Kyprianou, ☎ 25 42 17 51, 📠 25 42 18 75, 🖳 www.forestparkhotel.com.cy

• *MID-RANGE*

Pendeli (Map K–C3)

Comfortable accommodation, unpretentious and friendly.
✉ 12 Arch. Makarios Avenue, 4820, ☎ 25 42 17 36, 📠 25 42 18 08, 🖰 pendeli@cylink.com.cy
🖳 www.pendelihotel.com.cy

Edelweiss (Map K–C3)

Small, friendly, and good value for money.
✉ 53 Kalidonias, 4820 Platres Pano, ☎ 25 42 13 35, 📠 25 42 20 60, 🖳 www.edelweisshotel.com.cy

Agros

• *LUXURY*

Rodon (Map E–C4)

Efficient, comfortable, serves good food;

management are committed to ecotourism. Ideal for walkers and exploring Pitsylia.
✉ 1 Rodou Street, 4680, ☎ 25 52 12 01, 📠 25 52 12 35, 🖰 rodon@spidernet.com.cy
🖳 www.rodonhotel.com

• *BUDGET*

Vlachos (Map E–C4)

Cheap, clean and friendly; offers excellent buffet supper.
✉ 4680 Agros, ☎ 25 52 13 30, 📠 25 52 18 90.

Kakopetria

• *MID-RANGE*

Hellas (Map E–C4)

A small hotel, popular with Lefkosians.
✉ 4 Andrea Mamantos Street, Kakopetria, ☎ 22 92 24 50, 📠 22 92 22 27.

• *BUDGET*

Kifissia (Map E–C4)

Situated on the road to Agios Nikolaos tis Stegis – good value for money.
✉ 20 Aidonion Kakopetria, ☎ 22 92 24 21.

Pedoulas

• *MID-RANGE*

Churchill Pinewood Valley (Map K–B1)

This popular, comfortable resort offers hotel accomodation and self-catering apartments.
✉ PO Box 51626, 3507 Lemesos, ☎ 22 95 22 11, 📠 22 95 24 39, 🖰 pinewood@churchill.com.cy

• *BUDGET*

Marangos

(Map K–B1)

An old stone building with panoramic views. Comfortable, good value, but open only in July and August.
☎ 22 95 24 39.

Christy's Palace

(Map K–B1)

Located on the main commercial street; cheap, cheerful and open year-round.
☎ 22 95 26 55.

Krassochorio

Vasa (Map E–C5)

Tastefully renovated traditional village houses, in a friendly

village with a coffee shop and a bakery. Book through Sunvil Holidays in the UK.
⊠ Sunvil House, 7 & 8 Upper Square, Old Isleworth, Middlesex TW7 7BJ, ☎ (020) 8568-4499, 𝄞 (020) 8568-8330, 🖳 www.sunvil.co.uk

Lemesos
• *LUXURY*
Amathus Beach
(Map D–C1)
Well-established in extensive grounds; water sports and activities for children are on offer.
⊠ Amathous 4044, ☎ 25 83 20 00, 𝄞 25 32 74 94, ⌁ amathus@ spidernet.com.cy 🖳 www.amathushotel. com

Four Seasons
(Map D–B1)
Self-contained, with a kindergarten for children and superb pool.
⊠ Amathous, PO Box 57222, 3133, ☎ 25 85 80 00, 𝄞 25 31 08 87, ⌁ inquiries@ fourseasons.com.cy, 🖳 www. fourseasons.com.cy

Le Meridien
(Map D–C1)
Luxury resort, with three restaurants, a shopping arcade and a huge pool.
⊠ Amathous, ☎ 25 86 20 00, 𝄞 25 63 42 22, ⌁ reservations@ meridien-cyprus.com 🖳 www.lemeridien-cyprus.com

Elias Beach
(Map D–C1)
On beachfront, with the Parekkliste Village Country Club offering golf, bowls and riding.
⊠ PO Box 54300, Amathous, ☎ 25 63 60 00, 𝄞 25 63 53 00, ⌁ info@ eliasbeach.com, 🖳 www.eliasbeach. cy.net

• *MID-RANGE*
Avenida Beach
(Map D–C1)
A beachfront position in the Amathus district, where most other hotels rate five stars.
⊠ Amathous, PO Box 51500, ☎ 25 32 11 22, 𝄞 25 32 11 23, ⌁ avenida@ cytanet.com.cy

Continental
(Map C–B2)
Interesting 1920s building; lively and well patronized.
⊠ Spyrou Araouzou 137, ☎ 25 36 25 30, 𝄞 25 37 30 30.

Le Village (Map C–A1)
Friendly, comfortable, unpretentious family-run guest house.
⊠ 242 Leontios Archiepiskopou Street, ☎ 25 36 81 26, 𝄞 25 34 80 44.

• *BUDGET*
Hellas Guest House
(Map E–C5)
Old stone building in former Turkish district; cheap, clean, friendly.
⊠ Zig Zag 9, ☎ 25 36 38 41, 𝄞 25 31 80 59.

Exelsior Guest House (Map E–C5)
Friendly, cheap and cheerful.
⊠ Anexartisia 35, ☎ 25 35 33 51.

Pissouri
• *LUXURY*
Columbia Pissouri Beach (Map E–B5)
Superbly situated in a

bay with sandy beach and high white cliffs: good for water sports.
✉ Pissouri Bay, PO Box 54042, 3379 Lemesos, ☎ 25 22 12 01, 📠 25 22 15 05, 🖲 colombis@cytanet.com.cy
🖥 www.columbia-hotels.com

• **BUDGET**
Bunch of Grapes Inn (Map E–B5)
Restored farmhouse with courtyard. Peaceful, very good food.
✉ Box 59400, Pissouri, ☎ 25 22 12 75.

Kotzias Apartments
(Map E–B5)
Well-appointed apartments, with views over the bay.
✉ Box 59320, Pissouri, ☎ 25 22 10 14, 📠 25 22 24 49.

Larnaka
• **LUXURY**
Golden Bay Beach Hotel (Map H–C1)
Well-appointed hotel, all amenities, beach.
✉ Dekeleia Road, ☎ 24 64 54 44, 📠 24 64 54 51, 🖲 gbadmin@goldenbay.com.cy

Lordos Beach Hotel
(Map H–C1)
This is a large and friendly hotel – the beach offers a range of water sports.
✉ Dekeleia Road, ☎ 24 64 74 44, 📠 24 64 58 47, 🖲 administration@lordosbeach.com.cy
🖥 www.lordos.com.cy

Sun Hall Hotel
(Map G–C3)
This hotel is on the seafront – handy for the marina.
✉ 6 Athens Avenue, ☎ 24 65 33 41, 📠 24 65 27 17.

• **MID-RANGE**
Larco (Map E–F4)
In the old Turkish quarter – good value for money.
✉ Umm Haram Street, ☎ 24 65 70 06, 📠 24 65 91 68, 🖲 info@Larco-hotel.com.cy

• **BUDGET**
Harry's Inn
(Map E–F4)
Traditional house with nine charming rooms.
✉ Thermopylon 2, ☎ 24 65 44 53.

Agia Napa
• **LUXURY**
Grecian Bay Hotel
(Map J–B2)
Almost a coastal landmark, this hotel is situated on a superb sandy beach.
✉ PO Box 30006, ☎ 23 84 20 00, 📠 23 72 13 07, 🖲 grecian@grecian.com.cy
🖥 www.grecian.com.cy

Nissi Beach
(Map J–A2)
Nissi Beach offers bungalows, large pool and all the family facilities, including a babysitting service.
✉ PO Box 30010, ☎ 23 72 10 21, 📠 23 72 16 23, 🖲 nissi@nissi-beach.com.cy
🖥 www.nissi-beach.com

• **MID-RANGE**
Anesis Hotel and Apartments
(Map J–B2)
Located very close to Grecian Bay and the beach.
✉ PO Box 30370, ☎ 23 72 11 04, 📠 23 72 22 04.

Protaras

• Luxury

Capo Bay (Map J–C1)
Gardens overlooking
Fig Tree Bay.
✉ PO Box 33115, ☎
23 83 11 01, ☏ 23 83
11 10, ✆ capobay@
capobay.com.cy
💻 www.aeolos.com

Grecian Park Hotel
(Map E–G4)
This five-star hotel has
fine views, luxurious
rooms and a huge
lagoon-style swim-
ming pool.
✉ Cape Greco,
☎ 23 83 20 00,
💻 www.
grecianpark.com

Crystal Springs
(Map E–G4)
Far enough from town
to escape the crowds.
✉ PO Box 33246,
☎ 23 82 69 00,
☏ 23 82 69 01.

Vrissiana Beach
(Map J–C1)
Entertainment for the
children, and good
watersports facilities.
✉ PO Box 33029,
☎ 23 83 12 16,
☏ 23 83 12 21.

• Mid-range
Chrysland
(Map E–G4)
Away from the centre
with good in-house
facilities – the beach is
man-made.
✉ PO Box 239,
☎ 23 72 13 11, ☏ 23
72 12 68, 💻 www.
chryslandhotel.com.cy

Domniki Beach Apartments (Map E–G4)
Right on the coast –
close to Fig Tree Bay.
✉ PO Box 33493,
5314, ☎ 23 83 25 31.

Lefkosia

• Luxury
Cyprus Hilton
(Map E–E3)
The city's premier
hotel with facilities
(and price) to match.
✉ Leoforos Archie-
piskopou Makariou,
Box 22023, ☎ 22 37
77 77, ☏ 22 37 77 88.

Holiday Inn Lefkosia (Map F–A4)
Modern, comfortable
four-star in the centre
of the city, with pool.
✉ 70 Regaena Street,
☎ 22 71 27 12,
☏ 22 67 33 37,
💻 www.holiday-inn-
cyprus.com

Hilton Park Hotel
(Map F–A6)
Quiet surroundings,
200 rooms, huge pool,
extensive grounds,
and a choice of
restaurants and bars.
✉ Griva Dighenis,
☎ 22 69 51 11,
💻 www.hilton.com

• Mid-range
Cleopatra (Map F–A6)
Near main business
and commercial areas.
✉ 8 Florina Street,
☎ 22 84 40 00,
☏ 22 84 22 22.

Classic Hotel
(Map F–A4)
Just inside the walls
of the old quarter.
✉ Rigainis 94,
☎ 22 66 40 06,
💻 www.slh.com

Castelli (Map F–A4)
This refurbished hotel
good base for explor-
ing the old city.
✉ Ouzounian 38,
☎ 22 71 28 12,
✆ reservations@
kennedy-hotels.com

Vegetarian Food

The Greek word for vegetarian is *hortopha-gos* – 'grass eater' – which, of course, speaks volumes. Apparently vegetarian fare, such as pilaffs of bulgur wheat, may have been cooked in chicken stock. And even *koupepia/dolmas* (vine leaves stuffed with rice and pine nuts) sometimes include some minced meat in the Cypriot version – be sure to ask before ordering.

EATING OUT
What to Eat

Most people experience Cypriot food through endless alfresco meals: meat (*kebap or kleftiko*) or fish (grilled or fried), a large portion of *patates* (chips, with lemon juice rather than vinegar) and the ubiquitous *khoriatiki salata*, peasant salad like the Greek version but with the addition of pickled capers (*kapari/gebre*) complete with stems and leaves. Cypriot cuisine, sometimes hard to find outside a Cypriot home, has a heritage of interesting dishes, many of them vegetarian.

The **meze**, literally 'mixture', is an experience to be taken with a loose-fitting waistband – dishes (twenty or so) keep coming to the table, starting with dips and followed by a variety of dishes according to what is available. Better restaurants have realized that discerning visitors enjoy traditional Cypriot dishes, so nowadays more of these are beginning to appear in *mezedes* (starters).

Traditional Greek and Turkish dishes are almost identical in nature, and often very close in name. **Starters** can include *hummus* or *humus* (chick pea dip), *taramas* or *tarama* made with smoked cod's roe, *talatouri* or *cacik* (yoghurt with mint and cucumber)

tahine or *tahin* (creamy sesame paste with lemon), and *elies* or *zeytin*, consisting of green olives with crushed garlic and cracked coriander seeds.

'Peasant' **vegetable dishes** are often delicious stews, such as *louvia me kolokithakia* or *burulce* (black-eyed beans with courgettes in lemon juice and olive oil) and *bamies* or *bamya* (okra in tomato sauce). *Trahanas* or *tarhana* is a dried 'biscuit' of

bulgur wheat and yoghurt, added to soup with the local **cheese**, halloumi. For self-caterers, the quality of local vegetables in the south is superb. Wonderfully flavoured tomatoes, peppers, aubergines, artichokes and avocados abound.

Eggs (*avga* or *yumurta*) are often cooked in a sort of loose omelette using whatever happens to be in season. In autumn, this may be wild mushrooms; in spring, it could be thin wild asparagus or *strouthia* (which means 'little sparrows'), the leaves and shoots of bladder campion.

Fish tends to be quite expensive because catches around the island are rather small. Certainly worth trying are: *barbouuni* or *barbun* (grilled red mullet), *maridhes* or *gopes* (fried whitebait) and *xifia* (swordfish marinated in oil and lemon, and then grilled). Deep-fried squid (*kala marakia* or *kalamar*) are excellent when freshly caught, but most restaurant fare in Cyprus comes frozen from the Far East.

The expectation of **meat** at every meal has grown with prosperity and now meat is usually what hosts feel guests should be

Above: *Bread and salads are always good for a light summer lunch.*
Opposite: Souvlakia *(kebabs) are as much part of the holiday experience in Cyprus as the sunshine.*

Above: *The old buildings of Lefkosia's Laïki Geitonia have been restored, and now house shops and restaurants.*

Halloumi

For many visitors, *halloumi* (*hellim*) is their food discovery in Cyprus. This rather rubbery cheese is, like *feta* (*beyaz panir*), made from goat's or sheep's milk; mint is pressed into it and it is stored in its own whey. Cut in thin slices it can be eaten as it is, grilled or even fried for those with a contempt for calories. The super-market product is good but village *halloumi* is an experience not to be missed.

---

served. Meat dishes include *hiromeri* (cured ham), *keftedes* or *kofte* (meatballs), *loundza* (smoked pork), *souvlakia* or *şiş kebap* (grilled kebabs) and *sheftalia* or *şeftalia* (grilled sausages). *Kleftiko* or *küp kebap* is ostensibly lamb cooked for hours in its own juice in a sealed clay oven. This technique tenderizes even the most ancient sheep or goat meat. *Tavas* or *tava* is a stew made with beef or rabbit and lots of onions.

Cyprus has long been famous for its citrus **fruit**, but in season there are also apples, pears, apricots, peaches, nectarines, tiny bananas from the west, strawberries, grapes, figs, melons and pomegranates. The cherry season is short but well worth travelling to Cyprus for: try the traditional *glyka* – fruits in syrup.

Many **cakes** and **pastries** are seasonal, baked to accompany a religious festival, such as *flaounes* (a yeast turnover filled with raisins, eggs and cheese) for Easter and *vassilopitta* (yeast dough spread with egg, almonds and sesame seeds) for Christmas. Useful lunchtime or picnic standbys are pasties made with filo pastry: *tiropitta*, filled with minted cheese (either *feta* or *halloumi*), *spanachopitta* with spinach and cheese, or *eliopitta* with black olives. Cypriots have a sweet tooth and love pastries soaked in sugar syrup: *baklava* is nut-filled puff pastry, *daktila* are filo fingers with a nut and cinnamon filling, and *loukoumades* are deep-fried balls of choux pastry.

Honey, usually of the very runny kind, is a great favourite and is often served poured over creamy fresh yoghurt or with *anari*, a soft white cheese which is a by-product of *halloumi*-making. *Soutsoukou* is a long string of almonds coated by soaking in a concoction of grape juice, flour and rosewater and then dried. *Loukoumia* (Turkish delight, which is diplomatically called 'Cyprus delight' in the south) has long been a local speciality.

What to Drink

Freshly prepared fruit juices are readily available on the island. Water is also a great favourite: Cypriots take a connoisseur's attitude towards water from the mountains.

Several good (and cheap) **brandies** are produced, including a VSOP – this is a favourite tipple with locals in cafés. Visitors will probably encounter it as a 'brandy sour', virtually the national drink, mixed with ice, lemon juice, angostura bitters and soda water. Beware – in the heat, these slip down easily and rising from the table suddenly becomes a problem.

Ouzo (aniseed-flavoured spirit) is served locally with iced water and slices of cucumber. *Filfar* is an orange liqueur, marvellous as a nightcap. Visitors might be offered 'Cyprus

---

Some Wines of the South

Some well-known wines from major producers include:

WHITE

• **Aphrodite:** medium dry, full-bodied.

• **Arsinoë:** dry wine from Xynisteri grapes.

• **Bellapais:** lightly sparkling medium dry, particularly good accompaniment to a fish *meze*.

• **Palomino:** soft, dry; chill well before drinking.

• **St Pantelimon:** pleasant, medium sweet wine.

RED

• **Afames:** a reliable, full-bodied wine.

• **Cava:** a blend of Cabernet Sauvignon, Mataro and Shiraz from Pachna village.

• **Domaine d'Ahera:** lighter red, highly rated locally.

• **Othello:** good, dry red.

• **Semeli:** traditional, full-bodied red.

Well worth trying are wines from the smaller producers. Dry whites include: **Alina**, **Ambelida**, **La Noyere Laona** (based on the Xynisteri grape), or **Agios Andronikos** from Oellade. Reds include: **Agia Moni**, **Agios Antonios**, **Agios Elias**, **Ecological Winery** (dry special reserve), **Kilani Village**, **Laona**, **Pahna Village** and **Plakota**.

**How do you like
your coffee?**
In Cyprus you have two
alternatives. **Nescafé** is
a generic term for any
instant coffee, usually
served in a sachet with
a pot of tepid water for
do-it-yourselfers.
Traditional coffee, a
finely ground mocha
boiled in a small pot
and served unfiltered in
small cups, is called
Cyprus coffee. Those
with a sweet tooth
should ask for *kafés
glykos*; medium is
metrios and unsweet-
ened *sketos* or *pikros*
(the Turkish equivalents
are *sekerli*, *orta* and
sade, respectively). Local
connoisseurs recognize
intermediate stages.
Coffee is served with a
glass of cold water.

whiskey' in an assortment of 'pre-owned'
bottles – this is *zivania*, a fire-water. Treated
with care, it can restore life to frozen
extremities after winter walking or skiing,
either by being imbibed or as a rub. One
northern distillery produces *raki*.

Beers of the lager type are brewed on the
island: Carlsberg (under franchise) and Keo.

Mosaics in Pafos show that **wine** growing
and drinking have long been associated
with Aphrodite's isle, although you will
never see Cypriots the worse for wear in
public. The climate and soils are ideal for
viticulture: village wines, still obtainable
direct from huge terracotta vessels (*pithari*),
are of variable quality, the best being highly
quaffable. In recent years, young Australians
(often from *émigré* Cypriot families) have
imported the fastidiousness that Anti-
podean wine-makers use in their own
production, and Cyprus wine is rapidly
changing for the better. The dessert wine,
Commandaria, has long been famed.

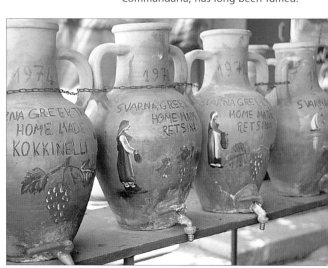

Traditionally, the main Cyprus grapes have always been Xynisteri (the native white grape) and Mavron (the black grape from Greece), but experiments are now being carried out with several others. North Cyprus has so far failed to produce any wines of quality, and most restaurant wine is imported from Turkey.

Cheap Cyprus **sherry** has an unfortunate image as the mainstay of the tippler. However, Cyprus dry sherries, served very cold, can take their place with the best.

Above: *Flowers are often used as a garnish at a buffet.*
Opposite: *Home-made* retsina, *served at the Svarna Tavern near Protaras.*

Where to Eat

In **Pafos**, fish tavernas sit side by side on the harbour and produce similar meals of good standard. Fish is locally caught (but chances are the squid is from Taiwan). Your custom will be solicited in friendly fashion.

Roadside Tavernas in the **Troödos** are usually quite cheap and cheerful and all serve much the same basic fare – dips to start, accompanied by village bread, then a meat course (*sheftalia* or *kleftiko*) with village salad. In the valleys, you can expect to find trout from the local farms.

In **Larnaka**, restaurants sit cheek-by-jowl along the Finikoudes and are much of a muchness – sit wherever you find a table. Flamingoes Restaurant Café at Hala Sultan Tekke serves good Cypriot fare. Located next to the salt lake, it is great for visiting naturalists recovering from a flight.

Wine Tours
Visitors to Lemesos can sample the local wines on daily guided tours of the various wineries and distilleries strung out along Franklin Roosevelt, the road from the harbour towards Akrotiri. The largest producer, KEO, lays on the best known trip (booking is essential in summer), taking in the **Commandaria** cellars, a *zivania* distillery, brandy and sherry. There is a final tasting session (and sales counter) with generous free samples: emerging into the light of day afterwards can prove a trying experience.

Pafos
Chez Alex

Not right on the seafront, but the fish is very fresh. Menu depends on the catch.
✉ *7 Constantia Street,* ☎ *26 23 47 67.*

Koh I Noor

For a change from Cypriot cooking, this is Pafos's best Indian restaurant.
✉ *7 Kleos Street,* ☎ *26 26 55 44.*

Phukhet

Serves very popular food cooked by Chinese chefs.
✉ *Tombs of the Kings Road,* ☎ *26 93 67 38.*

Tyrimos Fish Tavern

Family-owned seafood restaurant on the harbour, noted for its excellent fresh-caught fish dishes.
✉ *Agapinoros 71,* ☎ *26 94 28 46.*

North and West
Agios Georgios

A traditional coastal taverna overlooking the bay, serving good fresh fish.
✉ *Pegeia,* ☎ *26 62 13 06.*

Corallo Restaurant

International cuisine, made with quality ingredients.
✉ *Coral Bay, Pegeia,* ☎ *26 62 10 52.*

Pithary Tavern

A great favourite with the locals (both British expats and Cypriots); international menu.
✉ *Kissonerga,* ☎ *26 24 13 57.*

Villages near Pafos
Leda Village Tavern

Serves traditional Cypriot food.
✉ *Kouklia,* ☎ *26 43 23 11.*

Old Country Tavern

Situated on the road to Troödos via Agios Nikolaos, this is a lovely old stone building with traditional cooking. Some rooms available for an overnight stay.
✉ *Nikoklia,* ☎ *26 43 22 11.*

Kakopetria
Maryland at the Mill

Noted for its trout and spectacular setting on the banks of the river, this eatery is best visited after the lunchtime and afternoon trippers have departed.
☎ *22 92 25 36.*

Platres
Kaledonia

Unpretentious family restaurant with good traditional cooking. The *trachanas* soup is particularly welcome in cold weather.
✉ *31 Olympou, 4820 Platres Pano,* ☎ *25 42 14 04.*

Southern Troödos
Foini Tavern – Taste of Village

Unusually for a village restaurant, this one doesn't serve predictable traditional fare. It is popular, and many diners travel here all the way from Lemesos (which is a 30-minute drive).
☎ *25 42 18 28.*

Lania Taverna

Situated on the outskirts of a picturesque hill village, this eatery serves very good traditional food. Specialities include vegetarian meals prepared to order.
✉ 25 43 23 98.

Vasa Village Tavern

This tavern serves some of the best traditional food in Cyprus – including vegetarian dishes – with copious quantities of village wine.
✉ 25 24 28 63.

Lemesos

Al Pesto

An Italian-style meze restaurant that also serves traditional pasta, salads and excellent steaks.
✉ Opposite Limassol Amathus Hotel,
✆ 25 32 87 82.

Antonaros Tavern

This restaurant is popular, crowded and lively. No menu, just a superb meze.
✉ Attikis 5,
✆ 25 37 78 08.

Asterias Fish Tavern

A very popular fish taverna on the main road, serving a good variety of fish according to season.
✉ 55 Akademy Ave, Potamos tis Germasogeia, ✆ 25 32 65 66.

The Bay Tree

Serves the best of British home cooking, with dishes such as steak pie, beef stew, kippers and banoffee pie, all made using fresh local produce.
✉ Kanika Enaeiros Complex,
✆ 25 59 05 04.

Lefteris Tavern

A warren of small, usually crowded rooms in a village house; good food and a predominantly ex-pat clientele.
✉ Agias Christenis 4, Germasogeia,
✆ 25 32 52 11.

Neon Phaliron

Excellent traditional restaurant serving Mediterranean and Cypriot dishes.
✉ 135 Gladstonos,
✆ 25 36 57 68.

Nitayia Far East Restaurant

A stone warehouse with vast aquarium tanks around the walls; serves Thai, Japanese and Chinese food.
✉ 7 Saati, Old Port Roundabout,
✆ 25 36 06 71.

Ouzeri to Theseion

One of Lemesos's finest traditional meze spots, good for carnivores and vegetarians.
✉ Anexartisias 130,
✆ 25 34 77 44.

Porta Tavern

Meze, mixed grills, a good choice of vegetarian pasta dishes, and the house speciality – foukoutha, a do-it-yourself, fondue-style barbecue feast.
✉ 17 Genethliou Mitellas,
✆ 25 36 03 39.

Xydas

Modern fish restaurant with views over the town; somewhat pricey by Cypriot standards but certainly well worth a visit.
✉ Germasogeia

Tourist Area, Pantheas,
☎ *25 37 81 67.*

Pissouri
Bunch of Grapes

Popular with the service community, good food, but at a price.
✉ *Pissouri Village,*
☎ *25 22 12 75.*

Hani

Basically a transport café, serving very good Cypriot food.
✉ *On Lemesos–Pafos road,* ☎ *25 22 12 11.*

Larnaka
1900 Art Café

This trendy café-restaurant serves Cypriot food in an attractive old Larnaka town house.
✉ *Stassinou 6,*
☎ *24 65 30 27.*

Campanario Steak House

Good steaks and other grill dishes with tables in a tiny garden in summer. The wine list offers a good choice of Cypriot and Greek wines.
✉ *10 Nikodimou Mylona,*

☎ *24 62 61 10.*

Monte Carlo

Good Cypriot food – especially the meat *meze*. The balcony extends over the sea.
✉ *Piale Pasha 28,*
☎ *24 65 38 15 or 24 62 95 04.*

Pyla Tavern

Popular with families; serves fish in season, beautifully cooked.
✉ *Dekelia Road,*
☎ *24 65 39 90.*

Tudor Inn

Slightly more expensive than the norm, but the food is well cooked and presented.
✉ *28A Lala Mustafa Street,* ☎ *24 62 56 08.*

Agia Napa
Le Bistro d'Hier

Charming old house; serves superb international cuisine.
✉ *Odysseus Elytes 11,*
☎ *23 72 18 38.*

Protaras
Anemos Beach Restaurant

Good food, efficient service, great views.

✉ *7 Iasonos,*
5296 Paralimni,
☎ *23 83 14 88.*

Pixida Fish Restaurant

Wide menu of locally caught fish dishes.
✉ *5 Mendandrou,*
☎ *22 44 56 36.*

Vindobona

Unique in Cyprus – Viennese food accompanied by (taped) Viennese music.
✉ *On the main road to Agia Napa,*
☎ *23 83 14 48.*

Paralimni
Vangelis

Noisy, often crowded, this family restaurant is patronized by locals for its reasonably priced Cypriot food.
✉ *Griva Digeni Ave 40,* ☎ *23 82 14 56.*

Lefkosia
Abu Faysal

Informal and lively, this restaurant is housed in a fine old house with an art gallery. Authentic Lebanese cuisine is served to a cosmopolitan clientele.

✉ Klimentos 31,
☎ 22 36 03 53.

Aerikon

This meze restaurant is on the upper floor of the Bank of Cyprus building, with views across the old quarter of Lefkosia and the 'green line' – it is worth visiting just for the panorama.

✉ 86-90 Faneromenis,
☎ 22 84 81 98.

Astakos

This fish restaurant serves an excellent meze among other dishes; it is popular with the locals.

✉ Menelaos 6,
☎ 22 35 37 00.

Armenaki

An unpretentious restaurant that serves authentic Armenian dishes.

✉ Sans Souci 15,
☎ 22 49 83 16.

Chang's China Restaurant

Friendly and efficient Chinese restaurant – tables with rotating

centres make it popular for family outings.

✉ Acropolis 1, Engomi, ☎ 22 35 13 50.

Dikomo 74

This is a good spot for families, with a pleasant garden and Cypriot dishes from the traditional clay oven. The meze and kleftiko are both excellent.

✉ Metochiou 11,
☎ 22 78 17 28.

Fanous

This friendly, Lebanese-owned meze restaurant is in the heart of Laiki Yitonia, Lefkosia's picturesque old quarter.

✉ Solonos 7C,
☎ 22 66 66 63.

Hilton Hotel

The Cyprus Hilton holds 'International Speciality' evenings with generous buffets, for example 'Fish' or 'Cypriot'.

✉ Leoforos Archipiskopou Makariou,
☎ 22 46 40 40.

Irenias

An old taverna with

only 15 tables, serving what 'cognoscenti' regard as perhaps the best meze in Lefkosia – the bourekia in particular are legendary.

✉ Leoforos Archiepiskopou Kyprianou 64A, Strovolos,
☎ 22 42 28 60.

Konatzin

A very popular restaurant, known especially for its meze. Serves traditional and vegetarian fare.

✉ 10 Delfon,
☎ 22 77 69 90.

Mama's Kitchen

Traditional home-cooking from a take-away, with a menu that changes daily. Open at lunchtimes – including Sunday – it is deservedly popular, so expect to queue for your meal.

✉ Acropolis 44A,
☎ 22 31 26 55.

Navarino Lodge

A good buffet set out in a lovely garden.

✉ Navarino 1,
☎ 22 45 07 75.

Above: *Nightlife in Cyprus generally involves a fair amount of dancing.*

ENTERTAINMENT
Nightlife

There are two different kinds of nightlife in Cyprus. The strip in Lemesos and virtually all of Agia Napa is a sea of neon, with sophisticated nightclubs to rival any in Ibiza or Barcelona. These include something for all tastes, from sixties and seventies clubs to rave clubs to strip joints. Both resorts are fairly seasonal, more so Agia Napa. Lemesos is the best bet for out of season nightlife, as it is kept alive in winter by the conference market.

Then there are the bouzouki clubs, as favoured by Cypriot men. This is a completely different style of club and should not be missed; it involves a lot of traditional Greek dancing (with a Cypriot flavour), which becomes more complex and uninhibited towards the end of the evening and is huge fun. Some five-star hotels have a taverna in their grounds with bouzouki nights, where local entertainment, including plate smashing, is brought in. For anybody not into clubbing, all the resorts have a lively bar scene at night, with people bar-hopping late into the evening. In the villages, of course, the local taverna is likely to be the only nightspot. Lemesos also has cinemas

---

Lemesos Festivals

Lemesos has made a feature of a local love of festivals. In spring comes **Carnival**, with its grand parade and masquerade parties. In summer the **Lemesos Festival** attracts musical, dance and theatre groups from all over the world for performances in historic venues such as Kourion. In September there are the 10 nights of the **Wine Festival**.

---

and theatre, with films shown in English and occasional English theatrical performances.

Cyprus nightlife caters to a lively tourist trade. There are trendy discos and sophisticated nightclubs. There is ample opportunity to dine and dance under the stars and plenty of local atmosphere and fun.

Lemesos has a number of different cinemas scattered around the town all offering the latest films and the chance to enjoy freshly made popcorn with the film.

Theatre

As far as theatre goes, you have a good chance of seeing a Shakespearean play or a Greek drama performed in an ancient theatre by the light of the Cyprus full moon.

As well as enjoying a relaxing meal, Lemesos offers many different forms of evening entertainment with two attractive theatres – the Markideion and the Rialto that both host a variety of musical concerts as well as several dramatic events.

The **Kourion** Theatre in Lemesos (*see page 16*) was built in the 2nd century AD, restored in 1960 and can hold 3500 people for plays and concerts. One of Shakespeare's plays is staged every year at this theatre. The event is organized by the Committee for Chest Diseases, ☎ 25 36 30 15.

The Ancient Greek Drama festival is held every year by the Cyprus Theatre Organization (THOC) and the Cyprus Tourism Organization. The festival aims at reviving the glory of ancient Greek drama in theatres dating back to antiquity. Performances are mainly held at the ancient Kourion Amphitheatre and at other open-air theatres during July and August.

Lefkosia Municipal Theatre
It seats 1200 people and stages events throughout the year, including concerts and Greek language dramas. The Cyprus State Orchestra performs here.
✉ 4 Mouseiou Street, Lefkosia,
☎ 22 46 30 28.

Theatro Ena
Produces plays in Greek.
✉ 4 Athina Street, Kaimakli, Lefkosia,
☎ 22 34 82 03,
📠 22 34 42 70.

THOC New Stage Company
Performs works of Chekhov and Vaclav Havel, among others.
✉ Kampos Street, Lefkosia.

Kourion Amphitheatre
Classical and Shakespearean plays are staged in this amphitheatre, high on the cliffs overlooking the Mediterranean.
✉ 16km (10 miles) west of Lemesos.

Cyprus Centre of International Theatre Institute
✉ 38 Regaena Street, 1010 Lefkosia,
☎ 22 67 49 20,
📠 22 68 08 22,
🖥 ccoiti@cylink.com.cy
🕐 09:00–14:00

Traditional Music
Traditional folk songs
are often played in 7/8
time, and Cypriot musi-
cians cope easily with
changes between 2/4,
9/8, 5/8 and 6/8. Scales
correspond to the
Aeolian and Doric
modes used in the music
of the early church. In
the Orthodox church,
only chants are allowed;
the Armenian church,
on the other hand, has
a rich tradition of music
dating back to the 6th
century, much of which
is hauntingly beautiful.

Below: *A bouzouki
player: groups
performimg in large
hotels and res-
taurants include
traditional Cypriot
tunes in their
repertoire as well
as the inevitable
'Zorba's Dance'.*

Music and Dance

Young people in Cyprus, both north and
south, are as well-informed as any in the
western world about the various categories of rock and pop music. The national
radio stations play both Greek and Turkish
music. In the south, **traditional music** –
usually the light, rhythmical tunes of
tsiftetelis and *rembetiko* – is kept alive
by determined groups of musicians who
perform at weddings and various festivals,
or for dances.

Traditional **dances** are elegant, with an
emphasis on economy of movement, the
outstretched arms lending balance. Even
'gravitationally challenged' Cypriot men
can muster an instinctive grace which visitors roped in to dance find difficult to
match. Visitors are always encouraged to
join in traditional dances and everybody
will recognise tunes like 'Zorba the Greek'.
An evening of dance includes stunts like
balancing glasses on one's head and later,
demonstrations of plate-twirling, both of
which are extremely difficult.

Festivals

Easter is the major religious cele-bration of the year in Cyprus, when all members of the family join in together to celebrate. The date changes each year, but is 50 days after the first Sunday in Lent and it is an occasion for a carnival of its own. The main meal for Easter is *souvla* when the fast is broken and chunks of mouthwatering meat are roasted on a spit in the spring sunshine.

Above: *Traditional dancing frequently features as part of the entertainment in restaurants.*

Taken seriously by many Cypriots, **Lent** is a time when Christians all over the world stop consuming meat, fish and dairy prod-ucts for a period of 40 days.

Lemesos is famous for its Carnival cele-brations and processions. Look out for sea-sonal specialities such as pastry *bourekia* filled with mint-flavoured cheese and ravi-oli. Also sticky sweetmeats such as *daktyla* and *kandaifi*. Cypriots pack a picnic on this day and head for the countryside.

New Year's Day is called **St Basil's Day** in Cyprus. It is a day for optimism, when the people hope for a fruitful year ahead. A special cake, known as *Vasilopitta*, is made for the day. Whoever finds a coin in their slice is supposed to have good luck for the forthcoming year.

Epiphany is the day on which all Cypriots go to church to ask for a fruitful and prosperous year to come. Families gather and share a feast of mixed dishes. *Loukoumades* is the popular sweet of the day. At this time of year the citrus fruit is harvested and lorries loaded with oranges, tangerines, lemons and grapefruits make their way to the ports.

Holidays and Festivals

Many public holidays in the **south** are based on religious events and the dates depend on the church calendar:

1 January • New Year's Day
6 January • Epiphany
February/March • Green Monday
25 March • Greek National Day
1 April • Greek Cypriot National Day
April • Easter
1 May • Labour Day
May/June • Pentecost (Kataklysmos)
15 August • Assumption
1 October • Cyprus Independence Day
28 October • Greek National Day (Ohi Day)
25 December • Christmas Day

Above: *The Wine Festival in Lemesos lasts for 10 days.*

In September Lemesos holds a 10-day **Wine Festival** in its municipal gardens. There is plenty of entertainment each night, and visitors flock to the town in their thousands to enjoy all the fun. Wineries compete with extravagant stands, presenting grape pressings and hosting music and dance performances. Each evening, from 18:00–23:00, new wines are offered free to guests. There is plenty of international food to sample and the chance to try Cypriot dancing – while you tread grapes of course.

At **Christmas** time, every family used to slaughter a pig and the meat was salted, cured or smoked to last through the winter. Nowadays, Cypriot Christmas cake is the tradition, the basic recipe of which has been adapted to suit locals.

Nicosia Race Club
✉ 10–12 Grigori Afxentiou Street, Suite 102, Ayios Dometios, Lefkosia;
☎ 22 78 27 27;
📠 22 77 56 90;
📧 info@ nicosiaraceclub.com.cy
💻 www. nicosiaraceclub.com.cy

Cyprus Rally
📧 caa@ cytanet.com.cy
💻 www. cyprusrally.org.cy/
For accommodation, contact:
📧 yioula@ travelscope.com.cy

Gambling

There are no casinos in the Greek part of Cyprus as the Greek Orthodox Church does not allow casino gambling. There is a racecourse in Lefkosia which hosts 85 meetings a year, mainly on Wednesdays and Saturdays, with betting controlled by the Nicosia Race Club (*see* panel, this page).

Spectator Sports

The Cyprus Rally (*see* page 41) in Lemesos always interests both residents and visitors alike. The Rally Village is located at the shore, and everyone is able to mingle with the teams and their vehicles here, and then watch them in action at spectator points along the route.

Nightclubs
Lefkosia
Factory
Very good music at this club.

✉ 2 Michael Paridi Street,
☎ 99 44 65 88,
🕐 00:00–04:00
💰 CY£5.00

Scorpios
Mainstream music; this club is where the trendy people go.

✉ 3 Stasinou Street, Engomi, Lefkosia,
☎ 99 47 61 76,
💰 CY£4.00

To Treno
Enjoy the live music over weekends.

✉ 2 Yianni Koromia,
☎ 22 34 33 84,
🕐 Fri and Sat,
💰 CY£4.00

Lemesos
Romeos
Mainstream music played in an old warehouse.

✉ 23 Ariadnis Street, 4020 Lemesos,
☎ 25 31 38 23,
🕐 Fri, Sat and for special events,
💰 CY£5.00

Summer Liquid La Playa
A trendy deco nightclub, with an ancient theme.

✉ ex Les Palmiers Place,
☎ 99 46 06 02,
🕐 every night in summer,
💰 CY£5.00

Summer Privilege
Mainstream music and minimal-look decor. There is a pool in the centre and food is served.

☎ 25 31 43 43,
🕐 every night,
💰 CY£5.00

Pafos
Summer Cinema
Mainstream music and very trendy people.

✉ Yeroskepou,
🕐 Fri and Sat night,
💰 CY£5.00

Agia Napa
Abyss
A club with three levels and legendary foam parties on Fridays. Garage music is on offer.

🕐 00:00–04:00.

Gay Cyprus
There is no prominent gay scene in Cyprus, where machismo rules and the local people are not especially comfortable with homosexuality. Agia Napa is, however, one of the clubbing capitals of Europe and attitudes here are much more liberal. The resort is lively, mainly in the summer months.

Agia Napa
This town is rapidly become the most popular clubbing destination in Europe. Blessed with clear blue seas and lovely sandy beaches, it attracts not only the party crowd but sun seekers too. Visitors here can enjoy the scenery, the many water sports on offer, and for those who want to party, the choice is generous – the music ranging from retro to the very latest in house and garage.

Agia Napa also boasts a 16th-century monastery (*see* page 32) and archaeological remains, all in a scenic coastal setting.

Amnesia

Set low in the basement with a lounge upstairs. House and trance music.
🕐 *04:00–07:00.*

Carwash

An established club that has been given a makeover. Plays 70s and 80s music and features excellent sound and lighting.
✉ *Agias Mavris 24,*
☎ *23 72 13 88,*
✆ *info@ carwashdisco.com*
🕐 *00:00–04:00,*
💻 *www. carwashdisco.com*
💰 *CY£6.00*

Castle

A superclub with a castle theme, three separate rooms and a rooftop chillout terrace. There is trance and house music on Tuesdays, garage on Wednesdays and Fridays, and drum and bass also on Fridays.
✉ *Louca Louca 20,*
☎ *99 62 31 26,*
✆ *buzz@cylink.com.cy*
🕐 *00:00–04:00,*
💰 *CY£8.00*

Faces

A club with two levels and good lighting. House and garage music.
✉ *Louca Louca 20,*
🕐 *00:00–04:00,*
💰 *CY£6.00*

Gas

This club has everything: laser shows, smoke and bubble machines. House and garage music in one room and 70s and 80s music in another.
✉ *Makarios Avenue,*
☎ *99 68 41 95,*
🕐 *00:30–04:00,*
💰 *CY£8.00–10.00*

Grease

A trendy club in the heart of Agia Napa; 70s and 80s music.
✉ *Makariou Avenue,*
🕐 *00:30–04:00,*
💻 *www.3ds.com. cy.grease*
💰 *CY£8.00–10.00*

Insomnia

Garage music is on offer in this club for those who can't sleep. It is located just 10 minutes' walk from the square.

✉ Corner of Nissi Avenue,

🕐 00:30–08:00,

💻 www.3ds.com.cy/insomnia

💰 CY£4.00

Kool

This very successful club makes for an excellent night out, with its funky garage and disco house music.

✉ Makariou C,

☎ 99 62 31 26,

🕐 00:00–04:00.

P'zazz

This well-known nightclub has a capacity of 2000. House, garage, 70s and UK no 1 hits.

✉ 10 Kriou Nerou,

☎ 23 72 22 66,

✍ badtaste@lineone.com

🕐 00:00–04:00,

💰 CY£10.00

River Reggae

An open-air club surrounded by palms and other trees, with good reggae music for dancing.

🕐 04:00–07:00,

💰 CY£4.00

Emporium

An underground venue that holds as many as 1500 people and hosts some of the best DJs. Makes for a fun night out.

✉ Gregoris Afxentiou Street.

Mythology

This classy club is a popular hangout where the glamorous people go, so dress impressively. The music on offer is mainly house and garage, with a list of good DJs.

✉ The Square.

Below: Clubs and discos provide music, dancing and entertainment for every taste.

Right: *Four-wheel drive vehicles are ideal for exploring, but increased numbers could threaten the environment.*

EXCURSIONS

Cyprus is one destination where it really makes sense to hire a car, as the best sights are inland from the coast, or on remote roads not used by buses. Roads on the island are generally excellent, especially between the main towns, almost all of which is motorway. Mountain roads can be very slow, particularly if a lorry is ahead, which is often the case.

Pafos and Traditional Villages

(Route 1)

Take the coast road from **Pafos** west past Coral Bay and turn off towards the village of **Pegeia**. Here, you will find both good tavernas and ancient basilicas. Carry on into the hills towards **Kathikas**, **Ineia** and **Drouseia**, for spectacular views down over the coastal plain and across miles and miles of countryside – a sea of pink in February when the almond trees are in blossom. From Drouseia, the road descends towards **Polis**, a much quieter, less developed resort than Pafos, with some good tavernas right on the beach. Take a detour here along the coast to the well-known tourist spot, the **Baths of Aphrodite** (*see* page 40).

Pafos
Location: Map L–A2
(see also Map A)

Pafos Tourist Office
✉ Gladstonos 3,
CY 8046 Pafos
☎ 26 93 28 41
🕓 08:15–14:30 and
15:00–18:30 Mon–Sat,
closed on Wed and Sat
afternoons.

Pafos Forest (Route 2)

This trip is ideally taken from **Polis**. Take the road towards Stavros tis Psokas to **Lysos**, for a coffee stop in the ancient village square. Then head inland through the forest to **Stavros tis Psokas** itself, which is surrounded by beautiful, fragrant pine forests with marked walking trails. Before the village, climb up to the **Zacharou** vantage point for sweeping views of the north west coast, all the way to Akamas.

Polis
Location: Map L–A1

Polis Tourist Office
⊠ Vasileos Stasioikou 2, CY 8820 Polis Chrysochous
☎ 26 32 24 68
📠 26 32 13 27
🕘 09:00–13:00 and 14:30–17:30, Mon–Sat, closed on Wed and Sat afternoons.

Chrysorrogiatissa (Route 3)

Head from Stroumpi (Map L–A2) to the picturesque **Chrysorrogiatissa Monastery** and **Pano Panagia** village, birthplace of Archbishop Makarios. The monastery has spectacular views and sunset is a great time to visit. Wine and cheese tastings are organized here from time to time – the monks uphold an ancient tradition of winemaking and produce some great reds. If you visit during the day, take the road back to the coast via the tiny villages of **Statos** and **Pentalia**, emerging at **Timi**, near Pafos airport. On the road back into the town, there are some pottery shops worth a detour.

Below: *High on the spine of Akamas, Drouseia commands extensive views over a patchwork of orchards, vineyards and deep gorges.*

Troödos
Location: Map L–C2
(see also Map K)
Distance from
Lemesos: 47km
(29 miles)

Platres Tourist Office
✉ CY 4820 Platres
☎ 25 42 13 16
🕘 09:00–15:00
Mon–Sat, and
09:00–14:00 Sat.

Opposite: *Farmakas*
reservoir, enjoyed
by fishermen and
picnickers.
Below: *Kakopetria is*
a popular summer
resort for holidaying
Cypriots – out of
season, it is ideally
placed for exploring
the Troödos.

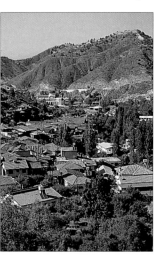

Troödos Hill Resorts (Route 4)

Arm yourself with one of the CTO's excellent walking tours brochures and head for the mountain village of **Pano Platres**. This is one of the main villages of the Troödos mountains, located on the southern slopes at 1200m (3937ft). Walking, cycling and painting are all popular pastimes here, and the area grows huge quantities of cherry trees. You can drive on to **Mount Olympus**, the island's highest point, meander around the many UNESCO-protected churches in the mountains, or indulge in a long lunch of mountain trout in a village taverna. There are plenty of gentle hikes. Platres is an ideal excursion on a hot summer's day, as it will usually be considerably cooler than the coast. In winter, however, there is often snow on the ground.

Around Pitsylia (Route 5)

View dramatic mountains and charming villages on an excursion taking you from **Agros** (Map L–C2) to **Palaichori**, and then up through **Farmakas** over a breathtaking pass down into **Odou**, on to **Eptagoneia**, **Kalo Chorio** and **Zoopigi**, and finally back to Agros. As with any small village, life centres around the church (as well as the taverna), and there are several interesting stops, including the 16th-century chapel in Palaichori. This excursion, however, is really a driving tour around the Troödos hill villages, so make plenty of stops along the way to explore the area on foot.

Ancient Kourion (Route 6)

Kourion is a half-day trip from Lemesos. Follow the coast road (not the new motorway) west out of Lemesos town to Kourion (*see* page 16), a beautifully preserved ancient **amphitheatre** dating from the 2nd century BC, with views of the sea. The stadium has been fully restored and is often used for theatrical and dance performances. Nearby **Kolossi Castle** was built in the 13th century by the Knights of St John and later inhabited by the Knights Templar. The castle today is in remarkable condition. Next, head inland to **Omodos**, one of the most famous wine producing villages – attractive, if somewhat commercialized. There's a monastery here containing some old icons and the small **National Struggle Museum**. Taste and buy wine and head back to the coast.

Pano Lefkara (Route 7)

Easily reached from either Lemesos or Larnaka, Pano Lefkara is the centre of the island's **lace-making** industry. A circular drive off the Lemesos–Larnaka highway includes

Ancient Kourion
Location: Map L–B3
(see also Map B)
Distance from
Lemesos: 19km
(11.8 miles)
⏱ 07:30–19:30 daily in summer, 07:30–17:00 daily in winter
☎ 25 99 50 48

Lemesos Tourist Offices
✉ ferry terminal, Lemesos Harbour
☎ 25 57 18 68

✉ Spyrou Araouzou 115A, CY 3036 Lemesos
☎ 25 36 27 56
📠 25 74 65 96

✉ Georgiou A 22, CY 4047 Lemesos
☎ 25 32 32 11
📠 25 74 65 96

⏱ 08:15–14:30 and 16:00–18:15 Jun–Aug, closed Tue and Fri. Times may change in winter.

Above: *Palm-lined Finikoudes Promenade in Larnaka is a popular place for evening strolls.*

the village of Vavla and also Lefkara itself, where you can wander around and admire the lace workshops, or stop for a coffee in the square. Nearby is **Choirokoitia**, an important Neolithic settlement on which houses have been reconstructed in the exact style of neolithic times. The same methods and materials have been used, and even the plants growing around the village are species dating back to the Stone Age.

Larnaka and Around (Route 8)

Larnaka on the surface appears to be a big, commercial town with little scenic beauty. There are, however, several interesting sites. The church of **Agios Lazaros** in the centre was built in the 9th century, restored in the 17th century and today represents one of the finest examples of Byzantine architecture in Cyprus. On the airport road, around Kiti, is **Hala Sultan Tekke** (*see* page 17), a very important mosque in the Muslim world, built over the tomb of Umm Haram, believed to be a relative of the prophet Mohammed. If you are spending the day in Larnaka, don't miss the **seafront promenade**, tastefully restored a few years ago and now an excellent spot for a fish lunch, as popular with locals and people on business lunches as with tourists.

Larnaka
Location: Map L–E2
(see also Map G)

Larnaka Tourist Information Offices
✉ Plateia Vasileos Pavlou, CY 6023 Larnaka
☎ 24 65 43 22

✉ Larnaka International Airport, CY 7130 Larnaka
☎ 24 64 35 76 or 24 64 35 77

🕐 08:15–14:30 and 15:00–18:30 Mon–Sat, closed on Wed and Sat afternoons.

Agia Napa (Route 9)

In the heart of all the bars and clubs of Agia Napa is a beautiful old **monastery**, built around AD1500, but with a cave inside it which suggests it may have been used as a much earlier place of worship. To the west of the resort, visit the **Makronissos Tombs** – 19 rock-carved tombs from the Hellenistic period. For some fresh air, drive to the southeastern tip of the area, to **Cape Greko**. Here, the stunning coastal scenery of towering cliffs and sea caves is enhanced by the fragrance of pine and juniper. Particularly impressive are the **Sea Palaces** between Limnara Beach and Cape Greko. These are a series of symmetrical rock sculptures hollowed into the cliff by the sea, overlooking water an incredible shade of turquoise. There are walks and scrambles around the Cape, although the paths do get busy in peak season.

> **Agia Napa**
> **Location:** Map L–F2
> (see also Map J)
>
> **Agia Napa Tourist Office**
> ✉ Leoforos Kryou Nerou 12, CY 5330 Agia Napa
> ☎ 23 72 17 96
> ⏰ 08:15–14:30 and 15:00–18:30 Mon–Sat, closed on Wed and Sat afternoons.

Theme Parks

Cyprus has a few unlikely theme parks. At Agios Ioannis Malountas, 25 minutes' drive from Lefkosia, is the **Ostrich Wonderland Theme Park**, one of Europe's largest ostrich farms (open Tue–Sun 08:30–19:30 in summer, 08:30–18:30 in winter). Larnaka has a **camel park** at Mazotos Village, where you can learn about camels and enjoy a ride. Off the Leoforos Nissi road at Agia Napa there's a **dinosaur park** with moving models and impressive sounds (open 11:00–13.00 and 16:00–24.00, Jun–Nov).

Below: *Children making friends with pelicans at Nissi Beach, Agia Napa.*

Above: *Popular Governor's Beach is now reached by a fast new road from Lefkosia.*

Island Fact File
Land area: 9282km² (3524 sq miles)
Greatest width: 95km (60 miles)
Length: 240km (150 miles)
Highest peaks:
Chionistra (Olympus) – 1952m (6404ft)
Madaris (Adelfi) – 1613m (5292ft)
Papoutsa – 1554m (5098ft)
Kionia – 1423m (4669ft)
Tripylos –1362m (4469ft)
Kykkos – 1318m (4324ft)
Nearest neighbours:
Syria – 95km (60 miles)
Turkey – 69km (43 miles)
Rhodes – 432km (270 miles)

Tourist Information

The **Cyprus Tourist Organization** (CTO) produces free accommodation directories, maps and brochures. CTO has offices in all large towns in the south of the island, at both airports and in Brussels, Frankfurt, Amsterdam, Tokyo, Paris, London and New York. 🖥 www.visitcyprus.org.cy

Entry Requirements

Nationals of the EC, Australia, Canada, New Zealand, the USA and many other countries do not require visas. Visitors are not allowed to take up any form of employment or do business: obtain the necessary details and documents prior to arrival from the Migration Department, Lefkosia, ☎ 22 30 31 38, 🖷 22 44 92 21. Passports must be valid for at least 3 months beyond the date of entry into the Republic of Cyprus. Visitors to the south are allowed to make two-day trips into the north (see page 49). Those holidaying in the north are not permitted, under any circumstances, to travel to the south.

Customs

Regulations permit duty-free import of up to 250g tobacco, 0.75l wine, 1l spirits, 150ml perfume and other items totalling CY£50. Cypriots arriving from visits abroad arrive laden, and foreigners are not often stopped. Cameras, laptops and the like – all clearly valuable – are not in practice a problem.
Cars: Visitors can obtain a permit at the port to import a vehicle

or three months free of taxes or duty, and can get further extensions of up to a year from the main Customs Office in Lefkosia. After this, a car can be kept only if full duty is paid and if the vehicle was less than two years old on arrival.

Health Requirements

No certificate of vaccination is required, and Cyprus is free of epidemic diseases: malaria, once a scourge, has been eradicated.

Getting There

By air: The main point of entry is Larnaka International Airport, ☎ 24 64 30 00. Pafos is a busy secondary airport, ☎ 24 42 28 35. Most scheduled flights are shared between Cyprus Airways and British Airways. Cyprus Airways' main office is at 21 Alkeou St, Lefkosia, ☎ 22 44 30 54, with branches in other towns.

By sea: Regular ferries connect Lemesos with Rhodes, Crete (Iraklion) and the Greek mainland (Piraeus, about 48hrs travel time). Prices vary according to season. Ferries from Ancona and Venice travel to Cyprus via Patras (mainland Greece); ferries from Bari and Brindisi go to Patras, whence transfer can be made by land to Piraeus for boats to Lemesos. Israel and Egypt are reached by ferry from Lemesos, Syria and Lebanon from Larnaka.

By car: The major ferries to Lemesos from Greece and Italy transport motor vehicles.

Getting Around

Buses: Long-distance buses run between major towns and cities at half-hour intervals, except on Sundays. Urban services run from 05:30 to 19:00, occasionally longer in the tourist season. Small operators connect villages and other communities – 'lorry bus' services may leave early for towns and return at the end of the working day.

Taxis: Service taxis, usually extended Mercedes accommodating 4–7 people, pick up by pre-arrangement at hotels and homes. They cost far less than private taxis, but do not cover airports. Rural Taxis are available in hill villages and resorts. In towns, taxi fares are metered (surcharge between 23:00 and 06:00 and for more than one piece of luggage over 13kg, or 29 pounds).

Road: If you want to **hire** a car, you must be over 21 years of age and hold a valid driver's licence (an international licence is not required). The large rental agencies are represented in most towns, at airports or through hotel reception, or book a car in advance through your travel agent. No mileage restrictions are imposed and **cheap diesel** is an important consideration when wavering between car or four-wheel drive. **Always pay for the collision damage waiver** – just a few pounds on the basic rental and well worth it – otherwise you could be liable for the first few hundred pounds in the event of a collision. Hire rates are very reasonable compared with elsewhere in Europe. Cars drive on the left, but taxi drivers sometimes forget and in the heat of summer people can be reckless. In towns and cities the **speed limit** is 50kph (30mph), on country roads 60kph (39mph) and on motorways 100kph (60mph). A **horn** sounded behind you (or as a car passes) is not aggressive, it means 'I am overtaking'. Sound your horn if approaching bends with poor visibility. All hired cars have red number plates and an extra 'Z' on the number – some resident drivers feel obliged to overtake any 'Z' car and if overtaken by a female visitor, male honour is slighted. Take care and, if in any doubt, don't overtake! Vehicles approaching from the right have right of way.

Hitchhiking: This is not generally favoured as a method of travel as it is so hot and dusty in summer, though villagers are very obliging. For young Cypriot conscripts surviving on a pittance of an allowance, it is a way of life.

Organized Tours: All hotels which participate in the package holiday trade offer day and half-day trips run by local companies in air-conditioned coaches with hotel pick-up.

What to Pack

In summer, lightweight cotton T-shirts and shorts suffice most of the time. In the mountains, summer evenings can be cold – pack a pullover and trousers. Sunhats and sunglasses make sense during the day. In more up-market hotels you might want more elegant clothes for evenings, but leave the tuxedo at home. In winter, some days might be shirt-sleeve weather while others call for a pullover and waterproofs.

Money Matters

The CY£ is strong and stable. It is subdivided into 100 cents. Notes are available in denominations of CY£1, 5, 10 and 20, and coins in 1, 2, 5, 10, 20 and 50 cents. Officially you can take out no more than CY£50; coming into Cyprus, sums above £500 should be declared (but few do so). Travellers' cheques can be imported without limit. At both airports, exchange is available for all flights. A low crime rate means that many people come to Cyprus with their national currency rather than travellers' cheques.

In the north the currency is the Turkish Lira, with its accompanying inflation. Many hotels accept CY£ as a foreign currency. Banks have inconvenient opening hours and red tape, and the rate is also better in exchange houses which change currencies without commission.

Cyprus intends to join the Euro in 2008, and from 2007 the Cyprus pound will be locked into a fixed conversion rate with the Euro in preparation for entry.

Credit cards: Plastic money is widely used. **VISA** (with PIN) can be used at Barclays and Cyprus Popular Bank. Cash is available on Access/Mastercard (over the counter) at Bank of Cyprus and National Bank of Greece. American Express has offices in Lefkosia, Lemesos and Larnaka. Many garages have pumps equipped to accept notes or cards.

Tipping: A 10% service charge is added onto hotel and restaurant bills, so tipping is not obligatory but small change is welcomed by taxi drivers, porters, waiters, etc.

Business Hours

Shops in tourist areas stay open late and all day on Sundays. Elsewhere, from May–Sep, shopping hours are: 08:00–13:00 and 16:00–19:00; Oct–Apr: 08:00–13:00 and 14:30–17:30; closed Wed, Sat afternoons and all day Sun. Public service hours: 07:30–14:30 Mon–Fri.

Banks: 08:15–12:30 Mon–Fri; and 15:00–17:30 in the main tourist areas.

Time Difference

Cyprus is two hours ahead of Greenwich Mean Time, one hour ahead of Central European Time, and seven hours ahead of US Eastern Standard Winter Time. Clocks go forward one hour on the last weekend

Getting Around

There is a single 'motorway' connecting Lemesos with Lefkosia and Larnaka: it ends at Erimi, west of Lemesos, and the volume of heavily laden lorries using the coast road to Pafos can make the going rather slow during the working day. Driving in Cyprus is further spiced by taxi drivers executing hair-raising moves in order to ply their trade.

Good fast roads connect the Troödos region with Lefkosia and Lemesos in the south, but these roads are also often congested by heavy lorries.

For the visitor with a hire car, a special attraction is the network of narrow cobbled roads weaving their way across the landscape, plus an even more extensive system of forestry roads leading well into the back of beyond.

After the winter rains, these roads can become quite heavily rutted and hard going even for four-wheel drive; by summer, many of them have been smoothed by the bulldozers of the forestry department skimming off the surface irregularities.

Insect Pests

Locusts migrating from North Africa are no longer the ravaging pests they once were. Early records of the British administration recount that everyone had to kill their quota of locusts and bring them to be weighed: failure meant fines or imprisonment. In the early days of British occupation many young soldiers died from malaria. Later, swamps were filled and eucalyptus trees planted to drain wet areas. These days, local **mosquitoes** are not malarial, but their infernal high-pitched whine can be maddening and some people are allergic to their bites. They are particularly vicious near the salt lakes, but they can be kept at bay indoors using small plug-in vaporizers.

in March, and back on the last Sunday in September.

Communications

Post: There are post offices in all towns, with poste restante facilities in the main offices. Postage stamps are also sold by newsagents. All letters sent to the **north** of Cyprus have to go via Turkey – the code 'Mersin 10, Turkey' must be added to the last line of the address.

Telephone: Cyprus is connected with 184 countries by direct dialling. **Directory enquiries:** dial 192 for local calls, and 194 for international calls. Cardphones and public payphones are widespread in all towns and villages, with dialling instructions in English and other languages. Telecards (CY£2, 5 or 10) can be purchased from banks, post offices, souvenir shops and kiosks. Off-peak reduced rates operate

for trunk calls between 20:00 and 07:00 and for international calls between 22:00 and 08:00 every day and all day on Sundays. Public faxing is not available, but virtually all hotels will send and receive faxes for their residents.

Electricity

The mains is 240 volts AC, supplied @ 50Hz. Plugs are standard square-pin or two-pin continental: adaptors are widely available in supermarkets and most other stores. Batteries (including alkaline and Ni-Cad) are manufactured locally or imported, and are available in all popular sizes at stores and garages.

Weights and Measures

The metric system has been used in the south since 1987, but some old Ottoman measures are still encountered: for weight the *oke*

(1.3kg or 2.8lb) and for land area the *dönüm* (1350m² or 0.33 acres). In the north, the mile is used for distances.

Health Precautions

Walkers, naturalists and other explorers should make sure that their **tetanus** protection is up to date. It is easy to underestimate the strength of the **sun** – even short exposure on sensitive skins can leave a child or adult in agony. Use sun hats, sun cream with a high protection factor (renewed after swimming) and practise sensible sunbathing. In the south, Cypriots are quite fanatical about health: fruit and vegetables are scrupulously washed and food and water supplies are monitored by a strict public health inspectorate. **Condoms** are readily available in most pharmacies (Greek *profilaktika*; Turkish *preservatif*).

Natural hazards: **Scorpions** are rare; large **millipedes** which sting are common, so check shoes and sleeping bags before use. The only truly venomous **snake** is the viper (*kufi*), for which anti-serum is available locally; the large black Montpellier snakes are harmless to humans. At the seaside, **weever fish** lie beneath the sand in shallow water with poisonous spines protruding. If you stand on one the pain is excruciating: put your foot in very hot water as quickly as possible and get medical attention. Colourful **ragworms** (black, white and red) sting when touched anywhere on their bodies. **Sea urchins** are a rather painful nuisance but they are not poisonous – wear flip-flops.

Medical Services

Medical care in Cyprus is available through government-run general hospitals or private clinics. In emergencies, all the general hospitals have **casualty departments** and provide treatment free of charge, but you should make sure your **travel insurance** policy covers any other eventualities. English is almost inevitably spoken extremely well since many Cypriot doctors will have trained in the UK, USA or Canada. Consulting hours for private doctors are 09:00–13:00 and 16:00–19:00 on weekdays. **Pharmacies** stock all branded medicines, many of which are available without prescription. Those pharmacies open late at night, on weekends and public holidays are listed in the newspapers.

Security

Cyprus is relatively crime-free. Until recently, **theft** from cars was unknown outside the Sovereign bases and most vehicles were left unlocked, but the incidence of theft from both cars and hotels has increased. The **police** are unarmed (except in the airports) and are quite helpful. In villages they are very much part of local life. English is widely spoken, so be polite if you are caught in a radar trap – your muttered insults will be understood. **Travel insurance** is generally available as part of a package, or can be pre-booked separately through your travel agent.

Emergencies

Dial **199** or **112** for emergency services such as an ambulance, fire service or the police. All-night pharmacies: dial **192**.

Etiquette

In monasteries and mosques visitors are expected to dress respectfully: no shorts or bare tops for men; women should cover arms or legs so as not to cause offence or be offended when admission to a place of worship is refused. It is also respectful to dress modestly when wandering around the villages, where the way of life is very traditional. Topless sunbathing is acceptable in hotels, however, and nude sunbathing is tolerated on Lara Beach on the Akamas Peninsula. It is strictly forbidden to remove any antiquities from Cyprus. It is also bad etiquette to the environment to pick flowers, drop litter and generally leave any trace of yourself.

Language

English is so widely spoken that it can be hard to practise your Greek (although people will always be very pleased if you try). In hotels, shops and restaurants, Cypriots usually have more than just a smattering of German, French, Italian and even Arabic.

Photography

There is no shortage of subjects in Cyprus for the landscape, architectural or wildlife photographer. As elsewhere in the Mediterranean, the light is of better quality in the spring and autumn months. In general, avoid taking photographs in the hours around midday. In the morning and evening, the longer shadows give better modelling and the slightly yellow light makes pictures warmer. Print film for your holiday snaps can be developed locally – there are outlets in all the towns. Film deteriorates quickly in the heat (especially transparency), so serious photographers are advised to bring their own film with them to Cyprus. Otherwise buy film only at places where you know there will be a quick turnover. Photography is forbidden near any military area.

Good Reading

Davies, P. & J. and Huxley, A. (1983) *Wild Orchids of Britain and Europe*. Chatto & Windus, London.

Durrell, Lawrence (1957) *Bitter Lemons*. Faber & Faber.

Georgiades, Christos Ch. (1989) *Nature of Cyprus*. Lefkosia.

Jonsson, Lars (1992) *Birds of Europe with North Africa and the Middle East*. Helm, London.

Karageorghis, Vassos (1982) *Cyprus from the Stone Age to the Romans*. Thames & Hudson, London.

Markides, Kyriakos (1977) *The Rise and Fall of the Cyprus Republic*. Yale UP.

Meikle, R.D. (1977) *The Flora of Cyprus*. Bentham Trust, Kew, London.

Oberling, Pierre (1983) *The Road to Bellapais: The Turkish Cypriot Exodus to Northern Cyprus*. Columbia UP, USA.

Pantelas et al (1993) *Cyprus Flora in Colour – The Endemics*. Lefkosia.

Stylianou, Andreas and Judith (1964) *The Painted Churches of Cyprus*. Trigraph, UK.

Thubron, Colin (1972) *Journey into Cyprus*. Penguin Viking.

Whalley, Paul (1981) *The Mitchell Beazley Pocket Guide to Butterflies*. Mitchell Beazley, London.

Maps: The CTO provides excellent free maps of major towns and tourist areas. On the rear of the Pafos map, there is a 1:100,000 map of the Akamas for walkers. Other more specialized maps are produced by the Department of Lands and Surveys in Lefkosia, including a Geological Map of Cyprus. The *Globetrotter Travel Map of Cyprus* is also available as a companion volume to this travel guide.

Useful Greek Phrases

yes • *né*
no • *ókhi*
hello • *khérete*
how are you? • *ti kánete?*
goodbye • *adio*
please • *parakaló*
thank you • *efkharistó*
sorry/excuse me • *signómi*
how much is? • *póso iné?*
when? • *poté?*
where? • *pou?*
I'd like • *thélo*
open • *aniktó*
closed • *kleistó*
one • *éna*
two • *dhio*
three • *tria*
four • *téssera*
five • *pénte*
six • *éxi*
seven • *eftá*
eight • *okhtó*
nine • *enniá*
ten • *dhéka*

INDEX OF SIGHTS

GENERAL INDEX

Page numbers given in **bold** type indicate photographs

GENERAL INDEX